Crime and Punishment in Dorset

A Thousand Years of Murder, Mayhem and Mystery

TERRY HEARING

DORSET BOOKS

First published in Great Britain in 2015
Copyright © Terry Hearing 2015

A CIP record for this title is available from the British Library

ISBN 978 1 871164 62 6

DORSET BOOKS
Dorset Books is a Partnership Between
Dorset County Council & Halsgrove

Halsgrove House, Ryelands Business Park,
Bagley Road, Wellington, Somerset TA21 9PZ
Tel: 01823 653777   Fax: 01823 216796
email: sales@halsgrove.com

Part of the Halsgrove group of companies.
Information on all Halsgrove titles is available at: www.halsgrove.com

Printed and bound in China by Toppan Leefung Printing Ltd

Contents

Acknowledgements

The author would like to express his appreciation of the support he received in the preparation of this book, and in particular to: Sam Johnson, Mark Forrest, Ed Bristow, Jo Hearton, Valerie Dicker, George Wickham, Steve Wallis, Neil MacFarlane, Margaret Hearing and Robert Hardy.

Illustrations appear by courtesy of the following:
Oxford Archaeology p 13
Shaftesbury Abbey Museum p 11
Dorset County Museum pp 18, 23, 25, 33, 42, 44, 48, 60, 61, 65, 74, 87, 91, 99, 100, 101, 115, 128, 135, 141
Dorset History Centre pp 9, 17, 19, 20, 33, 36, 37, 41, 43, 44, 45, 47, 56, 69, 89, 103, 105, 107, 114-5, 124, 129
The Brukenthal Museum, Romania p 26
Mr Geoffrey Sebag-Montefiore p 28
Mr J.N. Spencer p 30
National Maritime Museum, Greenwich p 53
Mr Neil MacFarlane p 64

Other colour photographs by the author
Author's Note: Sections 5 and 14 were first published in my booklet *More History on your Doostep* (2009), and a small amount of material from my book *Dorset Justice* (1999) is included in Part Two of this work.
If other copyright material has been used inadvertently, pardon is sought and apology made.
A correction will be made in any reprint.

Introduction

Crime is an enduring interest for most people. In fact or in fiction, 'naughtiness' at all levels intrigues humankind – not least because it is associated with mystery. A large proportion of popular entertainment is based on crime and its detection, and real crime in all its forms is rarely out of the news headlines. With all this attention, it might be imagined that we know a great deal about crime, but the truth is that we are woefully ignorant.

In the first place, the actual extent of crime is unknown. The most successful criminal is the one who not only escapes detection but who hides the fact that any crime has taken place. Some crimes go unreported by victims, though of course we do not know how many. The statistics of recorded crime are notoriously unreliable, and can be adapted by interested parties to prove either side of an argument. Trends in crime can be discerned, but broad conclusions are often fallible.

Secondly, the reduction of crime is a desired goal of public policy, often appearing impossible to achieve, and when it is achieved there appears to have been no one obvious cause.

Thirdly, there is not always universal agreement as to what is a criminal act. All that can be established is the interpretation of the law at a certain time by the criminal justice system.

A survey of Dorset crime over the last thousand years is subject to all the difficulties mentioned above, and the samples taken are chosen on the basis of interest and availability of information. Certain crimes are particularly relevant to Dorset as a rural and maritime county – you are not likely to find much piracy or poaching in an industrial city. However, most crime involves theft or violence or both, and in the aftermath of revelation can be seen as folly.

The book is divided into two parts: Part One is a chronological selection of individual occasions of crime, and Part Two is a survey of attempts to reduce crime.

Methods of dealing with crime have changed enormously and successively over the last two hundred years, and the last part of this book deals with punishment – retribution, deterrence and rehabilitation. It will be interesting to see if the statistical reduction in crime levels is maintained, or whether it is just a pause in the apparent inexorable rise of the last fifty years.

PART ONE

BEFORE 1600

*O*f course there was crime before 1600. The Anglo-Saxons before 1066 had codes of written law detailing offences and penalties, and the Normans who followed imposed their own legal system. Gradually during the Middle Ages the Common Law, the King's Courts, Baronial Courts, Justices of the Peace and Church Courts all developed to create a basis of law on which our modern system rests. Criminals were dealt with, and those who could not be caught were declared outlaws. Unfortunately, most courts did not keep records, and the records which were made rarely survived. What knowledge we have of crime in Dorset before 1600 rests mainly on incidental references, traditional stories and occasionally archaeology.

Domestic violence in the fifteenth century.

1. The Wicked Queen

A wicked stepmother, a handsome young king on horseback, a hilltop palace – and a savage murder so that the queen could put her own child on the throne of England: it sounds like a folktale, in which the true king would be miraculously saved by the Good Fairy.

Ordinary crime a thousand years ago left virtually no record. Law had developed among the Anglo-Saxon kingdoms, and when the Kingdom of Wessex came to dominance then gradually there came Common Law – common to the whole of England. However, justice was meted out by thegns and ealdormen, or in folk-moots, or by the king. Punishments were by local custom: for murder a financial penalty paid to the family of the victim was usual though not universal. Records were sparse – why should the details be written down when the interested parties were present and knew the decisions?

This explains why the only Dorset crime recorded for the tenth century AD is the murder of a king, and the accounts of it only appear second-hand and many years later.

King Edgar (959-975) had been regarded as a good king, maintaining his rule of England from his powerbase in Wessex with a light hand, supporting the Church and keeping the peace. The Danes who had settled in eastern England were happy to accept his suzerainty while he allowed them to govern themselves.

Edgar died suddenly, but apparently of natural causes. He left two sons, the elder of whom, Edward, was immediately recognised as king. Not all the nobles were pleased. Edward was reputed to have a violent temper, and had offended many who might have been his natural supporters.

Tenth century king.

8

Left: *Corfe Castle.*

Below left: *Corfe Castle in the eighteenth-century.*

Below: *A Victorian impression of Edward arriving.*

Edgar's widow Elfthryth was promoting the interests of her own son Ethelred, Edward's half-brother, who was still a young child. It seems likely that the rival factions of nobles came to blows, but Edward was crowned King.

Three years later King Edward was out hunting in Dorset when he decided to call on his stepmother and half-brother Ethelred at their residence in Corfe. According to an account written thirty years later, the king was seized by men supporting Queen Elfthryth while he was still in the saddle. Edward was stabbed to death – and there was no Good Fairy to resuscitate him.

The body of the king was hastily buried at Wareham, and Ethelred – later known in traditional history as Ethelred the Unready – was crowned king a month later. He was too young to have been implicated in the murder himself,

The site of Shaftesbury Abbey.

The leaden casket.

but there was general suspicion that his mother Elfthryth had planned it. Popular emotion surged, and Edward was dug up and taken to the nunnery at Shaftesbury, where his shrine became a centre of pilgrimage and miracles. Even King Ethelred himself came to recognise his murdered brother as Saint Edward the Martyr. There is no record of anyone paying the penalty for the crime.

The cult and veneration survived until the Dissolution of the Monasteries by Henry VIII, but a leaden casket strongly believed to have contained the bones of the saint is displayed in the Shaftesbury Abbey Museum.

When the monasteries were dissolved by Henry VIII in 1540, Shaftesbury was destroyed and the remains of St Edward were lost. Excavations by the archaeologist Wison-Claridge in 1931 revealed a leaden casket and later tests on the bones suggested that they could indeed be those of the murdered king.

Wilson-Claridge kept the bones in a bank vault in Woking, and eventually his wishes were respected and the relics were placed in the care of the Russian Orthodox Church Outside Russia. To this day they remain in a church in Brookwood Cemetery in Woking. A strange ending to a strange story!

2. Murder by a King?

Raids by Vikings are well-known in English folk lore and in popular history. It is easy to imagine the terror inspired by the longships, probing the estuaries for fat prey and loot, the berserks crashing onto the beaches in their terrifying helmets and swinging their battleaxes, while peaceful Saxon farmers and fishermen desperately tried to protect their families.

Scandinavian invasions of England were frequent from the late eighth century until 1066. Sometimes they were just raids, sometimes temporary settlements, but gradually there were permanent occupations and the conquest of the whole kingdom of England. It might be said that the invasion by William Duke of Normandy and the defeat of the last Saxon king Harold was the final success (at one remove) of the Vikings.

Throughout the period there were outrages and atrocities: Norwegians, Danes, Swedes and Anglo-Saxons were fierce in battle and cruel in revenge. The English King Ethelred, himself only king because his brother Edward had been murdered, was weak and unable to organise the defence of England against the apparently unstoppable tide of Danish immigration. In desperation he ordered that all Danes in the kingdom were to be killed. In the twenty-first century that would have made him guilty of a crime against humanity, but on 13 November in the year 1002 it resulted in the St Brice's Day Massacre. There is evidence that across the country his edict was obeyed by vengeful Saxons.

It is possible, though by no means certain, that a gruesome discovery in Dorset in 2009 is part of that evidence. Archaeologists working on the site of the new Dorchester to Weymouth Relief Road discovered a mass grave of more than fifty skeletons of young men. The bodies had been dismembered, and the skulls,

The mass grave of the Vikings.

12

rib-cages and leg-bones had been interred in separate piles. There were no obvious battlewounds, and the likelihood is that they were killed as captives. Further scientific analysis suggests that the victims had been beheaded from the front, and that they were of Scandinavian origin and dated to the 10th century.

Since no written record of this mass killing is known to exist, the field is wide open for possible explanations. Was this apparent atrocity due to the order of King Ethelred? If so, why were there no women, children and older men? Was this the extermination of a captured Danish raiding party which had landed in Weymouth Bay? If so, why were there no battle-wounds? It has been suggested that the execution by beheading from the front could have been a concession to the fierce warriors of the *Jomsvikings*, whose hard-fighting tradition was that all their wounds were taken to the front since they never retreated – but to be captured they must have been caught unawares and probably drunk!

3. Harry Paye – Arch-Pirate

The English Channel is a dangerous waterway. Nowadays the greatest danger is of collision because of the immense amount of traffic that passes through, and the intense supervision of the huge vessels by electronic means is essential. For many hundreds of years the danger came from bad weather, war and pirates.

Piracy – the stealing of a ship and its cargo – began when merchants first put out to sea. In the first century BC Julius Caesar himself was a victim and was held to ransom: he returned later and annihilated the pirates. Small trading communities were often both perpetrators and victims, and when European commerce developed in the twelfth and thirteenth centuries AD there were good profits in honest trade, and rich pickings for rogues. The little ports of Dorset began to flourish: Lyme Regis, Weymouth and Melcombe Regis, Swanage and Poole. When trade faltered, a foreign vessel proceeding up the Channel was a very tempting prey for the less virtuous shipmaster.

The Hundred Years War between the Kings of England and France beginning in 1337 provided even greater opportunity for skulduggery. For the English, it was now open season on French vessels, apart from the short periods when peace had been patched up. Unfortunately, the French felt the same way in reverse. Even during the periods of truce, predatory captains found it difficult to give up the habit and sometimes extended their range to the ships of countries not even involved in the War. Such information as we have comes largely from the recorded complaints of the victims to governments, which seem to have had little effect.

Henry Paye of Poole first comes to notice in English records in 1402, when he was one of fourteen individuals summoned to appear before the King's Privy Council to answer representations from the King of Castile in Spain, concerning the seizure of ships and goods belonging to subjects of that monarch. The record goes no further, but in May 1403 Harry Paye was summoned again, about the seizure of a ship called *St Anne* of Guerande in Britanny. In November the same year J. Drax was ordered to enquire into an allegation that Harry Paye had captured off the Isle of Wight a large ship (250 tons) with a cargo of iron belonging to merchants of Castile. Paye was ordered to return the ship, the cargo and the crew. His obedience may be doubted.

The season for maritime adventure in 1404 was very exciting. Paye first captured a vessel from Bilbao in Spain with a cargo of iron, two silver girdles and gold and silver with a value of 5000 nobles (about £1650 – a huge sum at the time and equivalent to several million pounds today). In the attack many Spaniards had been killed and wounded, and the survivors were put in a boat to row to the French coast. Yet another Spanish vessel yielded a value estimated at 12,500 nobles (more than £4000).

With relations between the English King Henry IV and the French King Charles VI deteriorating rapidly (the French were helping the Welsh who were in rebellion), Harry Paye was given authority to harass French shipping. In one engagement he was captured with his crew, and shackled on the deck of his own ship. Many of the French went below to plunder. Harry broke free, threw his guards overboard and killed the rest of the French as they emerged through the hatchway. Thereafter he sailed up the River Seine wearing a French flag, and looting many French ships as he went.

In 1405 Harry helped Henry IV against the Welsh rebel Owen Glendower, and then led an expedition against the ports of Normandy, burning 40 French towns and villages. This was too much, and a Franco-Spanish force descended on Poole while Harry was away. There was much destruction, and Harry's brother was killed.

The next two years saw him take his revenge, as he scourged the French shipping in the Channel and in port, as well as raiding northern Spain. It was said he took more than 120 prizes. All this was at a time when technically England was at peace with France and Spain, and therefore Harry was an arch-pirate.

Thereafter he seems to have retired, or at least to have kept his head down. Harry Paye died at Faversham in Kent in 1419, and his grave was marked with a memorial brass – but only the feet survive.

The memorial brass of Harry Paye.

A fourteenth-century ship.

4. Heresy and Atheism?

Sir Walter Raleigh.

On a fine summer evening in 1593, Sir George Trenchard hosted a strangely-mixed company of Dorset neighbours for supper at his great house Wolfeton just outside Dorchester. Wolfeton was in its heyday: an early Tudor manor house receiving a glorious late Elizabethan makeover with little expense spared. Grand staircase, long gallery, lofty ceilings decorated with exuberant strapwork – the house must have resounded for years with the hammering, sawing and imprecations of a host of workmen.

We know the names of the party-guests and some of their conversation from a report made to an Enquiry held at Cerne Abbas the following year at the behest of the Privy Council. The Council were worried by rumours that a group of gentlemen and clerics were spreading heresy and even atheism in both London and Dorset – and at the forefront was Sir Walter Raleigh.

An Elizabethan dinner party.

Raleigh was the archetypal Elizabethan adventurer, courtier, politician and freethinker. The admiration of the queen for his looks, personality and deeds had resulted in considerable wealth, including Sherborne Castle. He was also an intellectual, very well-read, and very willing to express views which might offend. Sir George might have known that there could be disputation over supper.

Wolfeton House.

Other guests included Raleigh's elder brother Carew, Sir Ralph Horsey of Clifton Maybank, John Fitzjames of Leweston, Roger Ironside the Vicar of Winterbourne Abbas, and Parson Whittle of Fordington.

The Raleighs may have dined too well, because towards the end of supper they began to quiz the clergymen about the nature of man's soul and the existence of God. This was dangerous talk at a time when religion was firmly controlled by all governments, and dissent from the official doctrine of the Church of England could easily be seen as treason. Carew Raleigh's comments indicate that he was out for trouble, showing little respect for Ironside's answers, and Sir Ralph Horsey remonstrated. Sir Walter Raleigh weighed in and told Ironside that he was no scholar, and this time Fitzjames attempted to support Ironside with a quotation from Aristotle. Sir Walter tried once more but would not accept

Ironside's answer, and called for Grace to be said to end the meal 'For that is better than this disputation'. And the two clerics promptly left!

Raleigh had enemies at Court and among his gentry neighbours. Never one to hide his contempt for lesser mortals as he perceived, and very much a self-made magnate who had traded on his favour with the queen, he was an easy target. Someone told the Privy Council about the supper party and an Enquiry was set up a few months later at the Nag's Head in Abbey Street, Cerne Abbas.

The Ecclesiastical Commissioners were looking into allegations of blasphemy, heresy and downright atheism, expressed not only at the supper party but in other places too. A stream of witnesses answered a series of basic questions: 'Whom do you know or have heard to be suspected of Atheism…? Whom do you know who hath spoken against God? Whom do you know who has said that the Scriptures are not to be believed?'

The witnesses were mainly clergymen who reported hearsay, but the Vicar of Blandford said that he had heard Carew Raleigh say that there was a God in Nature – a revelation of Paganism.

However, nothing came to light that could justify a charge against Sir Walter – the questions he had reportedly asked of Roger Ironside at the supper party could be described as legitimate theological discussion. The queen and her ministers certainly did not want Raleigh to be disgraced, and the Enquiry found nothing untoward. A few weeks later their trust in Raleigh was shown when he was sent to Chideock Castle to arrest a Catholic priest hidden there, a task for which he showed no reluctance.

It was dangerous to be an Elizabethan courtier, but Raleigh survived in spite of indiscretions. Bereft of royal protection after the queen's death, he spent fourteen years in the Tower writing great books of prose and poetry. Released for one disastrous voyage to the Indies, his death on the block was a political sacrifice for Spanish alliance by a cynical James I.

Queen Elizabeth I.

EARLY MODERN CRIME

The earliest court records in Dorset are those of Quarter Sessions. This meeting of Justices of the Peace for the County had been taking place four times a year for centuries, but the oldest account of their business begins in 1625. Much of what they did was what we would describe as Local Government, but some time was spent dealing with crime. The information recorded gives us some insight into mainly petty crime and punishment: most serious offences were tried in front of Judge and Jury at the twice-yearly Assizes. Further detail is provided by the personal Case Book kept by the Recorder of Dorchester Sir Francis Ashley. No records of the Petty Sessions held by local magistrates survive from this period.

5. The Wicked Lady of Martinstown?

In 1620 Alice Balston, a young servant girl, was accused of stealing 25 shillings from a chest in the 'old parlour' of her master's house in Martinstown. She returned 20 shillings to Mr Adred Paty, but had spent the rest. After examination by the magistrate Sir Francis Ashley, Alice was committed to Dorchester Prison for trial at the next Assizes. Theft of more than one shilling was a capital offence, so Alice was in grave danger. For a first offence, she might have been branded on the hand with the letter 'T' for 'Thief'.

However – six months later Sir Francis Ashley was examining her again. Alice had been to the great Woodbury Hill Fair near Bere Regis, held every September. Our nearest modern equivalent would be the Dorset County Show. Hundreds of stalls, booths and ramshackle temporary shelters were erected by tradesmen and merchants from across England.

Alice had too much to drink and slept in the 'bower' of Thomas Sowthey, on a pile of tanned leather hides, along with at least half-a-dozen others. According to her, she rejected the amorous advances of Thomas Gillett, a Dorchester shoemaker, until he offered her his purse – which she accepted, and then complied. Richard Ash of Fordington followed, and paid her 7 shillings. Gillett and Ash told a different story: they had been asleep and found their money missing in the morning. Neither man had had 'carnal knowledge' of the girl. The women present searched Alice and found 13s 3d in her shoe. Alice was again committed for trial at the next Assizes.

Once more she must have escaped the normal fate of such a miscreant, because in January 1621 Ashley was examining her afresh. She was pregnant, and explained her condition. On the day that she was released from gaol after the Assizes, a fellow inmate known as 'Long Robin' (also released) suggested that

Woodbury Hill Fair, early twentieth century.

they should go for a drink to Widow Peal's alehouse, and then to a house at Frome Whitfield, where they made love in the turfstore.

She may have been pregnant even before, because she said that the woman who acted as the gaol midwife advised her to name the father as her former employer Mr Paty – but she admitted that this was not true.

For the next few years Alice disappears from the records, until September 1624, when Sir Francis Ashley enjoyed her wild account, faithfully recorded in his casebook, of the riotous 'thieves' kitchen' at 'Boytherstonewood' alehouse. The details are extraordinary, with plentiful use of the 'cant' language mentioned in Elizabethan texts on the lives of vagrants and thieves. Alice appears to have become one of the homeless vagrant community, living by their wits and feared by law-abiding society. It is just possible that she made the whole thing up, but clearly Ashley was very entertained.

The following year Alice was again committed to the Assizes, with evidence from two gentlemen from Bradford Peverell, but then there is another gap of four years without mention. She re-appeared in 1629 at the Sherborne Quarter Sessions when Hugh Vyne, a small farmer of Dewlish, was bound over to obey a Bastardy Order in connection with her child. Soon after that Thomas Genge of Burleston was also bound over likewise – but this time the Order is in respect of 'Alice Balston, deceased'.

Was Alice a 'wicked lady', or a shameless hussy? Four hundred years later we like to think we are more compassionate, and so might consider that she could have been the victim of unscrupulous men, and of a society which had little sympathy or understanding of vulnerable people.

6. Dens of Iniquity in Early Seventeenth-Century Dorset

Aprominent County Justice of the Peace and Recorder of Dorchester, Sir Francis Ashley kept a 'Case Book' from 1614 until his death in 1635. The details of hundreds of crimes were noted either by Ashley himself or by his clerks, and show an underworld of society rarely glimpsed by historians. One examination of a witness in 1624 revealed the operation of a *'disorderlie house'* at *'Boythestonewood'* which may have been Boywood Farm near Mappowder. The witness was Alice Balston whose own criminal career might suggest unreliable evidence. However, the picture she gives of an alehouse frequented by Irish tinkers and local villains, where the customers arrived in the middle of the night demanding food and drink before taking umbrage and falling into a drunken brawl, and the landlord sought her out later to persuade her not to tell anyone: has the ring of truth about it. *'For (sayd he) if you doe I am undon.'*

The difficulty of keeping law and order in places where the legal authority was not clear was shown in Netherbury near Bridport in 1626. By a quirk of long-past lordship the two small settlements of Kingsland and Furley were within the parish of Netherbury but remained as a separated part of the *'Tithing'* (legal area) of Bradpole. This meant that the Tithingman of Bradpole (in effect the Constable) could not easily supervise Kingsland and Furley. The news got about and the population of the little hamlets began to swell with *'diverse poore people'*, who began to *'keepe unlicensed alehouses and have disorderlie meetinges, where (it is feared) manie stolen goodes are consumed to the great griefe and losse of manie theire honest neighbours.'* The magistrates sitting in Quarter Sessions ordered that from now on the Constable of Netherbury should have full authority to *'enter and execute his office aswell in Kingsland and Furley'*. Nothing further appears in the records.

John Browne, early seventeenth-century Dorset magistrate.

Alehouse scene, seventeenth century.

7. Soldiers Amok!

In 1626 England was at war with Spain and remnants of the army which had been sent to attack Cadiz the previous year were still roaming the countryside. Often unpaid, ill-disciplined, and unwilling to go home, over a thousand belonging to the regiment of the Earl of Essex were billeted in Dorset, according to the diary of William Whiteway of Dorchester. The notebook of the Recorder of Dorchester, Sir Francis Ashley, tells the story of one of their villainies.

Apparently about a dozen soldiers of Sergeant-Major Fryor's Company met a couple of local men in 'The Swan' at Evershot, and persuaded them to go *'to a Papist's howse to fetch out a Seminary preist'*. They all set off to find a house in Benvile owned by a Catholic family, the Breretons. This was a time when Catholics were regarded as potential traitors, and more particularly when England was at war with Spain. Catholic priests were automatically guilty of treason if found in England, as were those who gave them shelter. The plot was to search and plunder the house on pretence of looking for such a priest, or to extort money in return for going away.

Giles Fisher, a tapster at 'The Swan' offered to guide them. When they reached the house it was dark, and the soldiers stormed the house and one fired his musket into the hall. One of the two Brereton daughters, clearly terrified, threw out of the window the large sum of money of £4 10 shillings to *'forbeare the taking of any man out of the howse that night'*. The group then left and divided the money between them, spending most of it at an alehouse in Rampisham.

On a warrant from Sir John Strode, a Justice of the Peace, the soldiers were arrested and taken before him. Other soldiers *'assembled themselves together, threw stones in att the windows and attempted theire rescue, but prevayled not.'* Even so, the

Constable's attempt to march nine of the soldiers and the two local men to Dorchester must have been something of a pantomime, in that only four arrived at the prison. Later the suspects and witnesses were examined by Sir Francis Ashley, which is why we have the basic information.

According to William Whiteway, at least seven of the soldiers and the tapster of the alehouse were tried by a special Commission in January 1627, with Sir Francis Ashley as judge. All eight were condemned to death for burglary, but six of the soldiers were pardoned.

Benvile Manor.

8. Bastardy

In the seventeenth century it was an offence to produce a child out of wedlock, more particularly where this would result in mother and child becoming dependent on poor relief and therefore an expense to the parish ratepayer. The law was straightforward: both mother and putative father were to be punished by public whipping, the mother was to be incarcerated in the House of Correction for a year and the father was to contribute to the maintenance of the child. In practice the whipping was seldom applied, but mothers were held in the House of Correction when it was felt that firm moral training was necessary.

Mary Adams was released in the summer of 1637 because she had a 'loathsome disease' – but first she was publicly whipped in Dorchester where her bastard child was born and again in Litton Cheney where the child was conceived and where she used to live.

The business of establishing the identity of the father, pursuing him, making an order for maintenance, hearing the almost inevitable appeal and checking regular payments, occupied a great deal of magisterial time in and out of Sessions.

In April 1634 John Davie of Whitchurch appealed from the decision of two justices that he was the reputed father of the bastard child of Susan Tucker of Hawkchurch. She was said to have been *'a very lewd wench and hath been common to many'*. The appeal was allowed.

A judgment worthy of Solomon was given by the justices in 1632 when Thomas Hunt of Fordington appealed against the order to pay towards the upkeep of the bastard child of Ann Watts. He accused Thomas Tizard of being the real father.

After evidence was given, the court accepted his petition, but since both had had carnal knowledge, both were ordered to pay 6 pence a week.

John Dackombe, described as a gentleman, appealed in January 1630 against having to pay 8 pence a week for the bastard child of Joan Parker. Evidence was given that Joan Parker was in prison at the time of conception and John Dackombe was in London. Joan Parker had named four other fathers. Dackcombe, evidently a man of some means, had suspected a conspiracy against him and had petitioned the Privy Council in Star Chamber. Meantime the child had died, but the parish of Wimborne had to pay for its maintenance during life.

Punishment of mothers and putative fathers diminished, but even in 1754 three women were serving a year's imprisonment in the House of Correction and in 1771 Nathaniel Gundy was held in prison for want of sureties that he would pay for the upkeep of a bastard child in Cerne Abbas. The New Poor Law of 1834 established that mothers unable to support their children must enter the workhouse, while the parish officers had to try to get the money from the father. This applied to both married and unmarried mothers, and an enormous amount of effort and expense by the authorities has been made to enforce paternal responsibility. Until the end of the twentieth century most local prisons including Dorchester held men who had simply refused to pay, but this was recognized as having little success. A proper solution has yet to be found.

An honest citizen is falsely accused of bastardy, while the real culprit urges on the accuser (Hogarth).

9. 'Treason can but peep to what it would.'
(*Hamlet* Act IV Scene V)

When the Duke of Monmouth landed on the beach at Lyme Regis in June 1685 he was accompanied by a small force of soldiers. His standard of green and gold was raised, and although he did not immediately claim to be King, he was thereby guilty of High Treason. The local men who flocked to join him, crying for Protestantism and Freedom, were likewise guilty. The campaign through the West Country that followed ended in defeat and rout at Sedgemoor, and King James II duly took his revenge. The rebels who were not killed in battle were hunted down across Dorset and Somerset, and many were tried and executed including Monmouth himself. The fury of Judge Jeffreys as he sentenced men to be hanged drawn and quartered is still remembered after three hundred years.

Who were the rebels and what were they fighting against?

Monmouth himself was simply hoping to become King: and his previous history suggests he was unlikely to have been a 'good' king. The few gentry who had come with him were mainly down-at-heel adventurers, hoping for due reward. The crowds of recruits were artisans, craftsmen and small farmers, many of whom had suffered in recent hard times and who inevitably blamed 'the government'. The religious issue loomed large since James II made no secret of his determination to restore Catholicism whether Parliament liked it or not. The fathers and grandfathers of many rebels had fought on the side of Parliament against the Royalists in the Civil War, and considered the achievements which had survived the Restoration worth preserving.

The absence of the 'ruling classes' from the rebel ranks was significant. Whatever feelings they might have about King James, they did not see

Monmouth as a suitable replacement – and there was still the possibility that James might be brought to a more reasonable approach.

Many of the gentry did not hold to this view for long. About a year after Monmouth it seems there was a meeting at Charborough Park near Wimborne, hosted by Thomas Erle, at which a group of disaffected gentlemen planned a revolution. This meeting was shrouded in such secrecy (with good reason) that no details are available, and the evidence for it is a plaque on the wall which was placed there nearly a century after the event by one of Erle's descendants.

In 1688 James' determination to re-impose Catholicism and to ignore Parliament had become even more apparent, and the situation was compounded with the birth of his son and the prospect of a continuing line of Catholic monarchs. Seven leading members of the aristocracy signed an invitation to William of Orange to invade England and oust James – which he duly did.

The Duke of Monmouth.

Charborough Park.

Whatever happened at that meeting in Charborough Park, there is no evidence available that it influenced the 'Glorious Revolution', but the tradition is strong and this is proved by the plaque!

Plaque on the Icehouse at Charborough Park

UNDER THIS ROOF IN THE YEAR MDCLXXXVI
A SET OF PATRIOTIC GENTLEMEN
OF THIS NEIGHBOURHOOD
CONCERTED THE GREAT PLAN
OF
THE GLORIOUS REVOLUTION
WITH
THE IMMORTAL KING WILLIAM
TO WHOM WE OWE OUR DELIVERANCE
FROM POPERY AND SLAVERY
THE EXPULSION OF THE TYRANT RACE
OF STUARTS
THE RESTORATION OF OUR LIBERTIES
SECURITY OF OUR PROPERTIES
AND ESTABLISHMENT OF NATIONAL HONOR AND WEALTH
ENGLISHMEN
REMEMBER THIS GLORIOUS AERA
AND CONSIDER
THAT YOUR LIBERTIES PROCURED
BY THE VIRTUE OF YOUR ANCESTORS
MUST BE MAINTAINED BY YOURSELVES
THOMAS ERLE DRAX
ERECTED THIS STONE IN THE YEAR MDCCLXXX

10. Highway Robbery 1712

Single travellers were always at risk of robbery by footpads and highwaymen.

A brewer called Nathaniel Seager was travelling by horse from Shaftesbury to Blandford when he was stopped by a highwayman, who cried *"God damn you, you old dog, alight and deliver"*.

The highwayman not only robbed Seager but also attacked him with a sword, leaving him injured and bleeding. Soon after, Joseph Reader found the brewer lying on the ground, and was told what had happened. Reader, a well-built miller, ran after the highwayman in order to apprehend him. The highwayman fired his pistol at Reader, but the miller avoided being hit and felled the villain with his cudgel.

Reader was so incensed that he decided to carry out summary justice. Since the evidence was clear he had no difficulty in finding the prisoner guilty, and taking *'the Highway-Man's Belt from about his Middle, he put it about his Neck, and dragg'd him to a Tree, and fairly hung him up till he was Dead, Dead, Dead.'*

When the incident was reported to the Constable, Reader was arrested, brought before a Justice of the Peace, and committed to Dorchester Gaol to be tried for murder. Taking the law into your own hands was not popular with the authorities! Tried at the next Dorchester Assizes, Reader was shown a good deal of local support, and the evidence of the highwayman's victim Mr Seager easily persuaded the jury to acquit. The hat was passed round and the miller was presented with a goodwill gesture of thirty pounds – equivalent to at least eighteen months' wages.

11. Salvage (Portland Style)

The Wreck of the Abergavenny *1805.*

An enormous expansion of overseas trade between Western Europe and the rest of the world took place in the eighteenth century. A great deal of that trade passed up and down the English Channel. Careful and experienced though sailing captains might be, their ships were at the mercy of the weather, and it was all too easy to be driven into Lyme Bay by a strong south-westerly gale. Portland Race, a confluence of opposing strong tides, could make the control of a ship impossible, and the rocks of Portland Bill awaited – as did the wreckers.

Firmly embedded in the traditions of most coastal communities was the belief that what was cast on shore by the sea was available for collection by those lucky enough to find it. From at least the twelfth century this had been specifically denied in law, and in the eighteenth century the relevant Statute of 1713 was read out in coastal churches four times a year. 'Wrecking' as a crime included plundering wrecks and picking up items on the beach as well as the deliberate enticement of ships into danger.

Sometimes lords of the manor had been granted 'right of wreck' – the right to salvage – where their estate joined the coast, but it was commonly and erroneously assumed that this applied to anybody. This latter attitude was strongly held on Portland.

Portland was a separate community, isolated from the mainland, and linked only by a dangerous ferry pulled by a rope. The Portlanders were mostly very poor. Quarrying stone was the only industry, and agriculture difficult on infertile and windswept land. A wreck cast up on the island was 'manna from Heaven'.

It was the duty of Customs Officers to prevent 'wrecking' and to convey salvaged goods to a place of safety, such as the Customs Warehouse on Weymouth Quay. They seem to have been rarely successful, as a mob of islanders, scores or even hundreds strong, would strip a wreck in a very short time and would beat off official interference with volleys of stones. Casks of wine and brandy were particularly attractive, since they could be traded in Weymouth for the necessaries of life such as food and clothing which were so scarce among poor Portlanders.

Even when the cargo of a wreck was saved by the Customs men, there were still plenty of pickings. As the bodies of drowned sailors came up on the beach their clothes were ripped off and hidden. Sometimes there was more than a suspicion that the victims had not been quite dead, and were helped on their way. A large ship called the *Hope* was driven ashore on a January night in 1749, and broke up on the beach. In its hold was a chest of Spanish gold, gathered in the West Indies. Not many sailors escaped, and there was strong evidence – a stab wound – that one had been murdered. No-one was prosecuted.

Wreck site on Portland Beach.

Portlanders were thorough and efficient. A Customs Officer reported in 1742: *'We have caused a thorough Rummage in Chysell and other places in Portland adjoyning the place where the Ship was lost yet nothing of any value was found among the Inhabitants.'* Those who plundered were usually poor. Thomas Carter looted some tea in 1739, and was described by the Prosecution as *'in a Poore and Miserable condition with a wife and four children.'*

Wreck of HMS Meteor *on Portland 23 February 1830.*

12. Eighteenth Century Blackmail

The drama unfolds in a court report of 1756. William Bryer, as a Dorchester Borough magistrate, examined several witnesses in what appears to have been a case of attempted blackmail – though this is not specified. Five people gave their evidence on oath, and their words are recorded.

Betty Foy appeared on 14 January 1756 accused of attempting to extort money from a respectable clergyman, the Reverend Thomas Hayward. According to Betty, she and Mr Hayward had met at the Coach and Horses Alehouse in Fordington, but the landlord and his daughter Jane could not remember Mr Hayward, though Jane did remember a gentleman with Betty because the gentleman had given Jane a twopenny tip.

William Winzar, a clerk, says that he did know Betty Foy slightly, and he knew Mr Hayward. On Thursday of the week previous to the Court, Betty Foy had asked him to deliver a sealed letter to Mr Hayward. Winzar asked whether there was any harm in the letter. Betty said the letter concerned one Bet Vincent, and Winzar delivered it the next day, Friday. He says he did not know the contents of the letter nor who had written it.

On the next day, Saturday, Betty Foy told Winzar that she was three months pregnant by Mr Hayward, subsequent to their meeting at the Coach and Horses. On Sunday Winzar called on Mr Hayward at Betty's request and told him that if he did not come to a meeting with her then she would make the affair public. Mr Hayward treated the matter as a *'juggle and a contrivance to impose on him'*, and threatened to prosecute her for it. When Winzar told Betty she prevailed on him to write another letter in her name demanding a meeting at the Hole in the Wall Alehouse, with the further threat of exposure if Mr Hayward did not come.

Winzar and Betty then went to the Coach and Horses where the landlord told them that he remembered Betty being there with a gentleman but did not know who he was.

On Thursday 22 January Ann Hutchins gave evidence that the previous Friday (ie after the last hearing) she had met Elizabeth Foy at Mr Gundry's Corner. Betty had asked her what news there was in town, to which Ann had replied that the talk was all about Betty. Betty replied that those who talked about her were a *'parcel of Rogues Whores and Bitches'*, and that Betty was no more with child than Ann's basket of oysters that she was carrying. On the Tuesday after, Ann had again met Foy who declared publicly that she *'had sent Will Winzar to the parson with a Letter and that she had done it on purpose to get a little money out of him for that times were poor, but little money going and little Work to be done.'*

At the Court held the following day Friday 23 January James Chaffey the Mayor of the Borough of Dorchester presided, and heard the evidence of Lucy the wife of Nicholas Browne. Mrs Browne said that about a fortnight ago Betty Foy had asked her to write a letter on behalf of Elizabeth Vincent, saying that Vincent had lain with a gentleman at the Coach and Horses and was now pregnant. Foy told the witness that since Vincent *'was a fool of a whore and did not know how to talk with the gentleman'* the letter was to be written as from Betty, because she knew how to manage it.

The letter was to be taken by Will Winzar because as a clerk he had taken letters to Mr Hayward from the Rev. Mr Jacob, and therefore it would not be seen as unusual. Foy told Mrs Browne that she intended to demand ten pounds from Mr Hayward, which Bet Vincent could pay into the hands of the Parish authorities for the care of the child. The Parish would not then require the name of the putative father, who otherwise would be prosecuted.

Thus ends the report of court proceedings in this case.
What happened to Betty Foy?

The evidence suggests that Betty Foy was a young woman of doubtful virtue, who was capable of obtaining money by false pretences and even blackmail. She could not write, but could organise a scheme involving several people, who may not have known of her precise intentions. On the other hand she might have been entirely innocent – but it does not seem very likely! The evidence tells of an alehouse used for assignations, of women going about with baskets of oysters, of a clerk willing to run errands for young girls, and of a practice by which a putative father could avoid public humiliation by handing ten pounds to the parish authorities to cover the care of a bastard child.

Unfortunately the Offenders Book does not record whether the magistrates decided to commit for trial, and we do not know what happened to Betty Foy. She may have been the Betty Foy who was christened in Dorchester on 10 August 1735, and she may have been the Elizabeth Foy who was married in 1766.

13. Dorset Smugglers

In the year 1748 a little sailing cutter called *The Three Brothers* was fighting her way up Channel when she was sighted by a Customs Service patrol ship *Swift*, based at Poole. The cutter aroused suspicion, *Swift* gave chase, and after seven hours the cutter surrendered. Her cargo of brandy, tea and rum was clearly being smuggled, and was destined to be landed on a Hampshire beach to be collected by a notorious gang from Hawkhurst in Sussex.

Eighteenth-century Poole, a hotbed of smuggling.

The contraband was landed at Poole and stored in the Customs House on the Quay. After some months the Gang attempted to storm the Customs House but failed. Soon after a Sussex cobbler called Daniel Chater identified a friend as being a member of the Gang, and Chater was escorted across country by Customs Officer William Galley to give evidence to the Dorset magistrates. The two men put up for the night at an inn in Hampshire, and the landlady betrayed them to the Gang. Chater and Galley were seized, tortured with horsewhips, and murdered: Galley was buried alive in a sandpit and Chater was thrown down a well. In due course the story so horrified the locality that the Gang were themselves betrayed, arrested, tried and duly hanged.

Trade between countries or states has always been a source of revenue for governments. In return for permission to export or import, merchants have to pay tolls or duties, which they recover by charging more for the goods.

In the thirteenth century overseas trade across Europe increased substantially. After centuries of marauding Scandinavians throttling peaceful commerce, more settled conditions allowed the expansion of business: kings soon realised the potential.

It was King John in 1203 who first appointed Collectors of Customs at the main ports, and soon began the practice of 'farming-out' the customs on individual items to merchants who paid fees for the right to collect the dues. As might be imagined this was fraught with the opportunity for corruption, and often the government was forced to take back collection into its own hands. More and more goods were included on the lists liable for Customs duties. These lists were eventually laid out in a 'Book of Rates' in 1507. Under Queen Elizabeth I the first 'General Farm' was created to the benefit of Sir Thomas Smythe who paid to collect all the duties.

It goes without saying that corruption and smuggling must have been enormous, but the extent cannot be known. Attempts were made to improve the system in the 1650s under the Commonwealth, but in 1671 Charles II set up the Board of Customs with Commissioners whose duty was to enforce the collection. Gradually a service of Preventive Officers was established, but by the

Chater hanging at the Well in LADY HOLT, Park, the 'Bloody Villains standing by

The Bloody Smugglers flinging down Stones after they had flung his Dead Body into the Well.

Arish Mell, a cove frequently used by smugglers.

early eighteenth century the south coast of England was in what amounted to a permanent war between smugglers and Preventives.

From Lyme Regis to Poole the beaches and cliffs of Georgian Dorset were open invitations to the trade in contraband. The small numbers of Preventive patrols ashore and at sea meant that for most of the time the smugglers could go to work without hindrance: and what was more the onward transport by pack-pony or even wagon was safe enough with the secret connivance of the authorities and the mixture of bribery, fear of violence and general sympathy among the population.

Of course the actual volume of this illicit commerce can only be guessed. It is thought that by the 1770s most of the tea drunk in England had been smuggled. Other smuggling 'staples' included brandy, gin and tobacco, for which there was huge demand. Many other luxury items were profitable. Surprisingly, perhaps, even wool was smuggled from Ireland, a trade which probably reflected the burgeoning mechanised English cloth industry.

The principal sources of smuggled goods were the Channel Islands, where customs duties were not payable. Small ships, cutters or shallops, would cross during the day, mark an appropriate landing-place, and then deliver their

Poole Customs House.

Smugglers try to break in to the Customs House.

cargoes to the beaches when it was dark. Larger vessels would anchor off-shore and boats such as yawls would sail out to meet them. Sometimes barrels of brandy were put on rafts which were then sunk with heavy stones for later retrieval. If customs men were patrolling the area, watchers would light fires to warn the smugglers.

As business grew, so did the complexities of organisation. Many thousands of people were involved in some way with the sea-passage, landing, transport overland, protection and marketing of smuggled wares. When the eager consumers of contraband are taken into account, there can have been few people in Dorset not affected or implicated in some way. Honest businessmen must have wrung their hands in despair as their share of the market dwindled, and they were left with the choice of dealing with rogues or changing their occupation.

Smuggling seems to have developed what amounted to a secondary community, operating secretly and outside the law. Small individual enterprise grew into big business, receiving investment from pillars of the legitimate community such as landowners and merchants, who might even be Justices of the Peace. Successful sea-captains became employers of packhorse-teams and escorts, and worked through trusted agents to sell their goods in other parts of the country. At every stage of the operation there were those whose silence must be bought, with reward or threat. Violence hovered, and occasionally descended.

In the circumstances, it is amazing that authority continued to fight what must have seemed to be a losing battle. The Customs Service provided patrols by sea and land, could reward informers, and could call on the military for support when necessary – but the number of officers was small, the coastline extensive, and the ferocity of smuggling gangs was the subject of many stories in the alehouse. The case of Chater and Galley was perhaps the most notorious.

Occasionally a Customs officer would follow information and seize smuggled goods. As at Abbotsbury in 1720, he then had to face the local population who might prevent him from leaving the village. When officers attempted to search houses, villagers kidnapped the Constable and held him prisoner, knowing that it was unlawful for a Customs man to enter a house without the presence of an officer of the law. When successful seizures were made at sea or on land, the contraband goods were taken to secure warehouses at Weymouth or Poole. In due course the contents were sold by auction, but sometimes the warehouses were attacked by large gangs who were attempting to take back what they considered to be their own stock. Collusion between officers and smugglers was far from unknown. When a smuggling vessel was searched at sea in 1788, a detailed map and timetable of Customs patrols from Poole in the handwriting of the Deputy Controller was found in the captain's cabin.

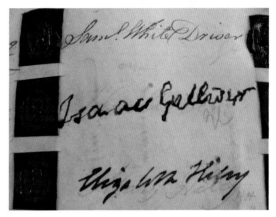

Isaac Gulliver's signature.

Some smugglers became very rich, and bought landed estates. Isaac Gulliver began humbly in his father-in-law's alehouse in Sixpenny Handley, and built up a business which in a few years became an illicit empire stretching along the whole Dorset coast. Clever investment in property, and an apparent determination to avoid violence in his criminal activity, enabled him to accept an amnesty to smugglers in 1782, and thereafter he appears to have led a respectable life. His final abode in West Boroughs in Wimborne remains to this day.

Some smugglers drank the alehouse dry, and died in poverty. Some lived modest but comfortable lives, and when caught by the authorities paid their large fines from their back pockets.

In the end, this profitable but illegal business died only when William Gladstone, Chancellor of the Exchequer in the 1850s, abolished most customs duties and established Free Trade, which lasted for the next eighty years.

14. Poaching

Poaching is a crime whose history is closely linked to the English class-system. Its roots can be traced to the Norman Conquest of 1066, when foreign baronial rule was imposed on the Anglo-Saxons. Whole areas of land were declared 'forest' where only the upper classes could hunt, and gradually the restrictions were extended to stop the peasantry from taking 'game' for the pot.

The definition of which animals, birds and fish were 'game' exercised Parliament particularly in the seventeenth and eighteenth centuries: there were no fewer than fifty-four Acts passed between 1660 and 1831. To protect the 'game' on their land the landowners employed an army of gamekeepers, whose privileges in law were first extended and then regulated by a Parliament dominated by their employers. After 1711 only one gamekeeper was permitted on each 'manor', and he had to be registered by the County magistrates – but when the need arose he could call on reinforcements to assist the arrest of poachers. Over a period of fourteen years in the eighteenth century more than two hundred gamekeepers were registered in the records of the Dorset Quarter Sessions.

To deter trespassers and poachers, 'man-traps' and 'spring-guns' were employed, and such implements are now displayed in museums across Dorset. It was not infrequent for entirely innocent individuals to be killed or maimed by them, and children were often their victims. The natural antipathy between rich and poor was made much worse by the whole issue of poaching and by the severe punishments, including transportation to Australia, meted out to ordinary people trying to feed their families.

Inevitably some poaching was much more criminal, and the poachers were organised in gangs who would come armed and prepared to tackle the gamekeepers. From 1693 poachers could be killed when found at night, and from

A gouty magistrate sits in judgment on a poacher caught on the magistrate's land.

1772 if found bearing arms they were liable to sentence of death. Such threats seem to have had little effect, since in 1780 occurred the notorious Battle of Chettle Common.

Cranborne Chase in North Dorset was a regular haunt of poachers, and both gamekeepers and poachers would venture into the woods armed and even armoured. Helmets made of straw bound with split bramble and jackets thickly quilted with canvas were favoured as protection against the staves wielded by gamekeepers – though this equipment was of little help against the slash of a keeper's cutlass. In 1780 on Chettle Common and in the dark hours of a December night a running battle took place in which a keeper was killed and another had his knee smashed by a poacher's swingle – normally used for beating hemp. The worst of the fight took place at what is still known as 'Bloody Shard Gate' and on into Bloodway Coppice. The leader of the poachers turned out to be a Sergeant of Dragoons called Blandford, and in the melee he had his hand cut off.

An armoured deer-hunter.

The trial which followed his capture was popular entertainment, with the crowd openly supporting and sympathising with the poachers. Blandford was sentenced to a short period of imprisonment, and his hand was buried at Pimperne with full military honours. Neither poaching nor soldiering is practical one-handed, and ex-Sergeant Blandford kept his half-pay, turned game-dealer, and set up business in London.

15. Antisocial Behaviour

In April 1632 William Goare was accused of living incontinently with a widow, Katherine Dyke. He had solicited other women and abused his own wife; according to Joan Pittman, wife of Thomas Pittman of Cattistock, he was drunk when he appeared at Blandford Sessions. The constable of the Hundred of Totcombe and Modbury, Robert Strode, had failed to execute the warrant for Goare's arrest. Goare, Dyke and Strode were all ordered to be of good behaviour and to appear at next Sessions. Goare was also fined 5 shillings for being drunk, and the fine was to go to the poor of Blandford Forum.

Travelling shows were always looked upon with suspicion by the authorities. In October 1630 a company of puppet-players arrived in Beaminster *'with certaine blasphemous shewes and sights'*. The Sands family, who were the players, operated by day and by night to *'the greivance of divers of the Inhabitants who cannot keepe their Children and servants in their houses by reason that they frequent the said shewes and sights late in the night in a disorderly manner.'*

Further, John Sands was said to have pursued the parish priest out of the church to argue about his sermon and to have brawled with a disorderly inhabitant. The players were ordered to leave the county by the following Monday and meanwhile to be of good behaviour.

Sabbath-breaking does not appear in the records as much as one might imagine, but in January 1630 the Constables of Wimborne Minster were ordered to levy a fine of 10 shillings on Eustace Moone for serving ale to Thomas Trendor and Hugh Quinioye on the Sabbath and in the time of divine prayer. Trendor and Quinioye were fined 3 shillings and 4 pence each.

Vagrants – people who had no regular home or employment – remained a source of concern to the justices and to Parliament throughout the centuries. It was assumed, often with good evidence, that wanderers were associated with crime and at the very least they were begging when they should be working.

Attempts were made to distinguish the rogues from the deserving, but generally vagrancy was met by local justices with whipping, return to place of settlement and incarceration in the House of Correction. Dorset Quarter Sessions in April 1728 (and in further years) supported these measures by funding 'vagrant carriers'. Richard Darke of Charmouth was to be paid £35 for the next year to carry vagrants by wagon out of West Dorset into Wiltshire, while John Pond had a similar responsibility for £20 in the east of the county.

Julian's Bridge, Wimborne.

In October 1755 at Bridport Matthew Powell of Wootton Fitzpaine was declared a vagrant and put on board a warship, and the tithingman (a constable) John Phelps, who arrested him, was paid £1 7s for his trouble . Frequently a wanderer could rely on a handout from an overseer of the poor, who would think it less bother than to prosecute, provided the vagrant moved on immediately.

The arrival of the Victorian workhouse, with no handouts, made life harder for wanderers, but even in 1869, Dorset Quarter Sessions expressed concern over the number of vagrants and it was suggested that a more rigorous policy of imprisonment should be adopted.

Occasionally a parish would appeal to Quarter Sessions for assistance in connection with an absconder. In October 1730 at Shaftesbury it was reported that John Cole of Chilfrome had abandoned his wife Elizabeth and had fled, leaving her to be maintained by the parish. Accordingly the overseers requested authority to seize his possessions which would be sold to make up some of the loss to parish funds. Cole's furniture and stores are listed and valued, to a total of £2 19s, while his land was assessed at 40s.

Joseph Downton was remanded in custody in October 1754 *'for running away and leaving his wife and children to the parish of Leigh and also by one other Mittimus [Court Order] bearing date 21st day of September charged on oath being the Father of a Male Bastard Child born of the body of Mary Whiffen of Leigh aforesaid and for his refusing to find Sureties for his appearance at the next Sessions.'*

As trade across the country increased in the late eighteenth and early nineteenth centuries, so did the construction of bridges. In Dorset John Dyson was appointed County Engineer, and made a survey of bridges in July 1809. The following year he reported that *'Evil Disposed persons'* were *'throwing Plank into the Stour'* at Blandford, and the magistrates offered a reward to informers. In the 1830s vandalism against bridges must have alarmed the authorities, since iron plates were installed warning that offenders would be liable to transportation for life.

Bridge warning, Sturminster Newton.

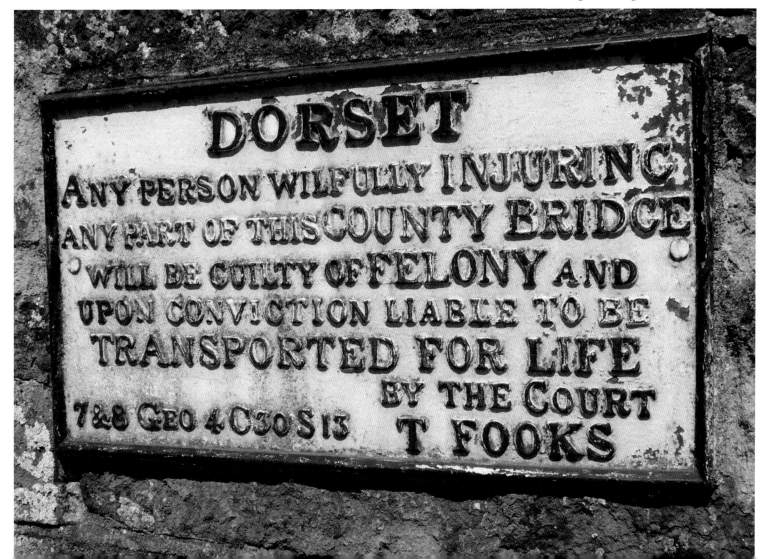

CRIME IN THE NINETEENTH CENTURY

*D*orset remained predominantly rural and maritime in the nineteenth century, and crime associated with the growth of industrial cities played little part. There were fears that the railway might bring urban villains in search of easy pickings, but these fears were largely unrealised. Poverty and deprivation show through in crimes such as turnip-stealing; smuggling and poaching continued as problems until the mid-century; petty violence appears more often in the newspapers. Strong middle-class demand for reform led to many initiatives for crime reduction and a more constructive approach to punishment. A problem specific to the countryside was the drunkenness in the harvest field, based on the traditional issue of copious cider to the harvesters. This frequently led to violence or accidents, fully reported in the local press.

16. Not Guilty? The Portland Press Gang

Recruitment to the sailing Royal Navy was often difficult, especially in war-time when the fleet expanded to meet the emergency. The impressment of sailors by naval captains in need could be authorised by a magistrate within his jurisdiction. This usually meant that a squad from the ship would search a port for men who *'used the sea'*, and forcibly take them on board. In fact the rules were often broken, and untrained *'landsmen'* were snatched from the streets. Press gangs were feared and hated by coastal communities.

In the spring of 1803 Napoleon Bonaparte refused the diplomatic terms offered by the British government in a brief lull in the long war between the United

The Press Gang – cartoon by Gillray.

The Sailor's Return – a survivor of the press gang?

Kingdom and France. He began preparations for invading England, and the British Admiralty in turn looked once more to the necessary plans for naval defence. This meant a rapid recruitment of sailors.

On 3 April 1803 the British frigate *Aigle* was in Portland Roads, moored by Portland Castle, and was under orders to raise men by the press to be taken to Portsmouth. Captain George Wolfe sought authority from the Mayor of Weymouth and Melcombe Regis to conduct a *'press'*, and this was granted. The Mayor was legally a magistrate for his year of office, but his writ was confined to the limits of the borough, which did not include Portland. Presumably the naval captain did not realise this, because he led a press gang ashore on to the Island.

Aigle was a new 600-ton ship of 36 guns, built at Bucklers Hard in Hampshire in 1801. Her complement was about 250 officers, sailors and Royal Marines. The press gang included 27 Royal Marines armed with muskets, some seamen with cutlasses and four officers with pistols.

Almost immediately a Portlander called Nicholas Way was seized and taken back to the ship, but released soon afterwards because he was the captain of a small vessel and therefore exempt under the rules. This was a very disappointing haul for the first day, and Captain Wolfe resolved to do better the next morning. The gang was ashore by the Castle at dawn and caught Henry Wiggatt and then Richard Way in Chiswell, as many of the villagers fled up the hill. The Constable of Portland Castle then challenged Captain Wolfe, pointing out that his warrant from the Mayor of Weymouth had no authority on Portland. Wolfe brushed him aside and the gang pushed on up the hill and down to Easton Square.

Frigate

The Dorset Coast.

By now the Portlanders had gathered in force in the Square and the mood was ugly. Muskets were produced and may have been fired. Nevertheless Wolfe's men seized Richard Bennett, the crowd pushed forward to rescue him, and Wolfe fired his pistol into the ground. The Lieutenant of Marines took this as a signal to open fire, and a volley of musketry killed three men immediately and others were severely wounded. The evidence is rather vague, but it seems likely that muskets were discharged from doorways, injuring sailors and Marines, but then the mob dispersed. Among the casualties was Mary Way, a young girl fatally hurt whose tombstone in St George's churchyard is pointed out to this day. The press gang returned to the ship.

At the inquest which followed the Coroner returned a verdict of Wilful Murder on the bodies of the three Portland men. In due course Captain Wolfe and three of his officers were charged and lodged in Dorchester Gaol to await trial. At the Summer Assizes in 1804 they were acquitted, on grounds of self-defence.

17. Sheep-stealing

To steal a sheep – or two, or more – must always have seemed an easy crime to commit. With the flocks roaming broad pastures, farmers often unsure of numbers, shepherds unable to watch effectively at night: a surreptitious snatch and the slash of a knife could bring good profit from an unscrupulous butcher, or it could feed a starving family for a month.

Dorset supported huge numbers of sheep on the chalk hills and in the lush valleys at many stages of history. Daniel Defoe's famous estimate in 1700 of six hundred thousand sheep within a 10-mile radius of Dorchester may well have been an underestimate. Three hundred years earlier the Abbot of Milton Abbey was using his expected woolcrops over years as collateral for a loan to rebuild his church. Three hundred years after Defoe the hills are again crowded with the sheep of farmers taking advantage of high prices being paid by oil-rich Middle-Eastern states.

Dorset Horn sheep.

It is not surprising that court records have plenty of evidence of sheep-stealing: and the thieves on the record as always are the ones who failed.

The earliest surviving Dorset record of what must have been a commonplace crime appears in the Quarter Sessions Order Book for January 1635, when Ambrose Piddle was sentenced to be whipped for stealing a white wether (a ram) worth eleven pence. The value is important since a figure of twelve pence or more would have made it a capital crime, and this may well have been an undervaluation to save Piddle's life. Three months later Nicholas Grant was convicted of stealing five ewes and a wether with a total value of 19 shillings and fourpence, and he was hanged. Such a sentence by magistrates was rare, and almost all capital offences were tried in front of a Judge at the Dorchester Assizes – but the Assize records from the early seventeenth century have not survived.

Sheep on the Dorset Hills.

For the next hundred years it seems likely (without comprehensive records) that casual sheep-stealing by individuals for consumption or sale continued, with occasional outbreaks of large-scale rustling by gangs based in towns. The beginning of the punishment of transportation to the American colonies provided a useful alternative to hanging, and a rather stronger deterrent than branding on the hand. This latter was applied when the miscreant pleaded 'benefit of clergy', the ancient legal fiction by which it was assumed that a first-time offender was a cleric who could not be punished by loss of life or limb.

In 1741 the situation changed dramatically following an outbreak of rustling in the pastures just outside London. Outraged graziers who were supplying meat to a burgeoning metropolis petitioned Parliament and a Bill was rushed through: sheep-stealing was made an immediate capital offence without benefit of clergy. The result was a flowing stream of death sentences for the next ninety years. Many were commuted to transportation, but across the country there were hangings for sheep-stealing in each of those ninety years, until the Act was repealed in 1832. The numbers in Dorset were not as great as might be expected, but executions tended to coincide with years of particular hardship: for example in the lean times of 1801 John Foot was hanged outside Dorchester Gaol.

Transportees for sheep-stealing tended to be aged between twenty and forty. Some were family men, like Thomas Kiddle of Longford, who was married with six children and was sentenced to seven years in Van Dieman's Land (Australia) in 1830. One twenty-three year-old, William Smith of Sydling St Nicholas, was sentenced to death in 1827 for stealing one sheep, though this was commuted to transportation for life. He had been a shepherd for Mr Hugh Sty at Godmanston, caring for 800 sheep.

Towards the middle of the nineteenth century there were more frequent cases where transportees awaiting shipment and imprisoned in the 'hulks' moored at Portsmouth and Bristol, were pronounced unfit and released in England in due course. When transportation ended, sheep-stealers were likely to serve terms of imprisonment according to the seriousness of the crime. Sheep-stealing still goes on, of course, largely by town-based gangs with a known market, and to the great detriment of farmers

18. Bread or Blood

James Frampton.

The condition of the 'labouring poor' in the countryside grew steadily worse in the early nineteenth century. Wages for farm labourers lagged well behind the rising cost of food during the long French wars, and afterwards the release of many soldiers and sailors on to the labour market made the situation worse.

Fearful of popular 'Revolution', the ruling classes combined fierce repression with an extension of the Poor Law to subsidise low wages with an allowance based on the price of bread and the size of a family. This resulted in yet more misery and the demoralisation of country labourers, since no matter how hard or how long they worked, they were always dependent on hand-outs.

When farmers began to use machines to thresh the harvested corn, and thereby deprived day-labourers of their winter employment, this proved to be the last straw. Across southern England from Kent to Dorset, in the second half of 1830 there spread a series of protest riots, machine-breaking and rick-burning, supposedly led and inspired by a mythical 'Captain Swing'. The contagion reached Dorset in late November.

The magistrate and landowner James Frampton faced a mob at Winfrith, and read the Riot Act. Under the law, once this had been done and the crowd had been ordered to disperse, an hour had to elapse before the military could be called in to enforce order. As it happened Frampton had been present in Paris at the beginning of the French Revolution, and all his life he was aware of the dangers of mob violence. In the event his house at Moreton was not stormed. A man and two boys were arrested at Bere Regis.

On 26 November William Coward's threshing-machine was destroyed at Woolland by a riotous mob from Stoke Wake and Mappowder. They then

Moreton House.

demanded money from farmer Christopher Morey, and smashed a machine at Buckland Newton. A local vicar attempted to appease them, but they pressed home their demand for higher wages. The following day farmer John Young at Pulham was forced to give money to the rioters to encourage them to leave peacefully.

Two days after that a farmer at Stour Provost who was also a Constable was attacked by a crowd, but surprisingly managed to capture some of them. These he carted off to Shaftesbury intending to put them in the lock-up. Clearly the lock-up was not in frequent use, since nobody could find the keys, and the prisoners took the opportunity to escape.

Further trouble occurred at Lulworth, Preston, Wool, Stalbridge and Lytchett Matravers, including rioting and machine-breaking. However, it was noticed that not all rioters were labourers, and the motives of some were far from clear. General protest and the excitement of creating mayhem certainly played their parts. One participant turned out to be a farmer and part-time beer-shop keeper, and it was assumed that he had stirred up trouble in the hope of increasing his liquor business.

Altogether there was more threat than violence in Dorset compared with some other counties. It was noted that while the rioters at Buckland Newton were carrying pistols they made no attempt to use them even when attacked by light cavalry carrying lances. There was some nocturnal rick-burning, but mainly arson was threatened rather than carried out. By early December the trouble petered out.

In January 1831 came the reckoning. Some sixty men and boys were arrested and tried in the Shire Hall at Dorchester. Six men convicted of demanding money with menaces were sentenced to death, as the law required at that time. In due course those sentences were commuted to transportation to Tasmania for seven years. A further six were also transported, fifteen more sent to prison for various terms, and a surprising thirty acquitted – which suggests that juries were not anxious to condemn.

One other result was that some debate took place among farmers, landowners and the clergy as to the desirability of increasing wages. It was, however, at best half-hearted; and four years later occurred the trial of the Tolpuddle labourers, ostensibly for swearing an illegal oath but really for trade union activities. It was their 'martyrdom' and transportation to Australia which really began the very slow improvement in the conditions of agricultural workers.

19. Town and Country Arson

The fear of fire in both town and country was very great before the arrival of modern equipment and prevention. Accidental fires were frequent, and if the circumstances were right could spread rapidly destroying towns and produce and of course lives. Since many buildings were wooden or had wooden frames they were easily combustible. Consequently deliberate acts of arson were regarded with horror, and severe punishment was demanded.

In the country aggrieved farm labourers had resorted to arson both individually and in gangs when driven desperate by farmers who they thought had mistreated them. The changes in agriculture of the eighteenth and nineteenth centuries in search of the profits to be found in feeding an increasing population had meant evictions, lower wages and unemployment – and from time to time resentment led to rick-burning and even the mutilation of livestock. Sometimes such brute protests were widespread, as in the 'Swing Riots' of 1830; at others there were single expressions of powerless frustration, as in the case of Joseph Way.

Way was a farm labourer in Milborne St Andrew in 1846 who had been dismissed. Drowning his sorrows in the 'Oak' public house he joined others in commenting on a strange light in the evening sky. His assertion that it was a fire was proved right when it was discovered that a barley rick was ablaze, and soon afterwards a wheat rick went up as well. Some of Way's drunken remarks occasioned suspicion. He was arrested, found guilty of arson at the Assizes in Dorchester and sentenced to transportation for life. Not long before he might well have been hanged, but in the previous few years death sentences had been severely reduced.

Silvester Wilkins was not so lucky. In 1833 he was sixteen years old, and in an act of bravado to show off to his mates in Bridport he set fire to the thatch of his father's neighbour. The building was a combing-shop where the tangled fibres of hemp were separated preparatory being made into rope. It burned merrily, and no fewer than eight properties were destroyed. At this time the memories of the Swing Riots were very recent, and in spite of his youth the full rigour of the then law was applied. Silvester was hanged on the roof of the gatehouse of Dorchester Prison.

Dorchester Prison gate.

20. The Great Dorset Mail Robbery

The Night Mail was ambling along towards Bere Regis on a moonlit night in 1844. The Blandford and Puddletown mail cart had just the driver and a horse, and carried three mail bags – this was the very early days of the new Penny Post, and correspondence was increasing. The mail from London came down by Royal Mail Coach through Salisbury to Blandford and Dorchester.

Suddenly two men jumped over a field gate and attacked. One man held the horse's bridle, and a pistol was brandished as the driver was knocked over and searched. The bags were grabbed and the men ran off. The empty bags were found next morning, and at Blandford it was estimated that at least 35 shillings (£1.35) had been stolen – not perhaps the haul the robbers had hoped.

Consideration of the usual suspects resulted in the arrest of James Baker, who steadily refused to name his accomplice. Found guilty at the Dorset Assizes, Baker was sentenced to transportation for life, but was later found to be medically unfit and was sent to the fearful Millbank Prison in London.

Three years later the railway from Southampton and London reached Dorchester, and the Puddletown mail was distributed from there.

A nineteenth-century post office mail cart.

21. Soldiers Amok – Again

An Irish navvy and the 11th Hussars.

In the year 1858 there were two groups of feisty young men abroad on the streets of Dorchester.

A year earlier the Great Western Railway had completed its broad-gauge line from Bristol down to Weymouth, relying on the brute strength of hundreds of Irish navvies to throw up the embankments and dig out the cuttings. Although the trains were running there was still plenty of work reinforcing and improving the track, and the navvies lived coarse and primitive lives in makeshift camps. Proud of their strength and eager to spend their pay they flocked into towns, and in Dorchester they found the 'Mariners' Inn'. Women were to be found there as well as beer.

Another band of muscular youth were the 11th Hussars, a cavalry regiment housed in Dorchester Barracks. They also were proud – and were unique in the British Army in that they wore crimson trousers. Only a few years earlier they had charged the Russian guns with the Light Brigade at Balaclava. They too sought women and ale in the 'Mariners' on a February evening, and found the Irish already there. The result was inevitable.

The battle was fierce, with the navvies wielding their shillelaghs or cudgels, and the cavalrymen their whips. Shillelaghs were more effective and the soldiers retreated up the High Street fighting off the savage attacks of the Irish. Having only a couple of Constables available, the Superintendent of Police hastily sent an appeal to the barracks for assistance, but the soldiers who arrived brought their swords and joined in against the navvies. Bloodshed followed, and other people passing by were caught up and injured. The melee continued for hours until the combatants were exhausted.

The following day the regiment was confined to barracks, but no such discipline was available for the Irish!

22. A Turnip Bandit

Dorset County Chronicle
Thursday 7 April 1864:

Dorchester. County Petty Sessions. Saturday.

'Mary Jane Morris was summoned for stealing a quantity of turnip greens, valued at 1d., the property of Mr James Lovelace, of Piddlehinton, on 26th of March. The case was proved by P.C. Hann, who saw the defendant taking the greens. She admitted the fact, but said she took them because she was in want. Fined 10s and allowed a fortnight to pay, or in default seven days' imprisonment. Mr Lovelace afterwards applied to the Bench to mitigate the sentence, as he did not wish to press the case. The defendant, after being cautioned, was therefore only fined 1s 6d, including costs.'

NB A fine of 10 shillings was equivalent to a week's wages for a labourer – perhaps £300 today.

Turnip greens.

23. Dangerous People in Sixpenny Handley...

Dorset County Chronicle
Thursday, 20 March 1879:
Wimborne. Petty Sessions.

'James Case, a noted poacher, and the ringleader of the trespassers on Lord Rivers' preserves, was charged with having on the previous day assaulted P.C. Hann and threatened his life. The Deputy Chief Constable stated that Hutchings' wife was summoned before the Cranborne magistrates on a charge of assaulting one of the young men who was defendant in the last case, and there was such a strong feeling against him that he ordered Hann to accompany him home. The offence was committed on the way. P.C. Hann said: "About four o'clock yesterday I was walking from Cranborne in company with Walter Hutchings to Handley. When I got about a mile from Handley I passed Case lying by the side of the road on the down. He began halloaing 'Jinnett,' and Hutchings stopped to speak to him. I said 'Come on, Hutchings, don't stop to speak to him.' Case then jumped up and came after me, and said 'I'll serve thee as they served Cox.' I walked on between 30 and 40 yards, and he came up and said I had searched him on the highway. He then took off his jacket and offered to fight me. I called for Hutchings to come on, and Case then came behind me, took me by the collar, and threw me down with great force on the ground. When I got up he struck me in the mouth with his fist, and then took a knife out of his pocket and said 'Life for life.' I succeeded in getting the knife from him before he could open it, and struck him down with my staff. I then endeavoured to take him into custody. He was very violent, and I sent Hutchings for a horse and cart and conveyed him to Cranborne." Prisoner denied he took out his knife till after the constable struck him with his staff. The magistrates considered the case to be most serious, and remarked some stops must be adopted to check the lawlessness of the people of Handley. Prisoner was sentenced to four months' hard labour.'

A Victorian drawing of Sixpenny Handley after a fire.

24. Abandoning a Moving Locomotive

In December 1899 Percy Nutman was driving a train on the line from Weymouth to Portland. The fireman, Frank Willis, was busy shovelling coal into the firebox when, just after the train had crossed the old wooden viaduct known as the Weymouth Backwater, he realised that Mr Nutman was no longer on board. His consternation can be imagined! Frank Willis was only eighteen years old and had been a fireman for six weeks – not long enough to learn much about engine-driving. However, he managed to stop the train in Rodwell Station.

It seemed most likely that Mr Nutman had fallen or jumped as they crossed the harbour, but no trace of him was found. Before paying Mrs Nutman the compensation due to her for what might have been an industrial accident the Great Western Railway made enquiries, and discovered the train-driver living with his sister-in-law in Surrey.

Train about to cross the Weymouth Backwater.

Weymouth Viaduct.

Nutman was duly charged with leaving his engine whereby there could have been public danger, and in due course he was sentenced to six months' imprisonment.

Forty-two years earlier, in January 1857, a train left Dorchester with a line of wagons carrying heavy wooden sleepers. The line had not been opened to the public, and Weymouth Station was still under construction. Just as the train entered Bincombe Tunnel the driver realised that the regulator controlling the speed of the engine had jammed and it was gathering speed down the long incline into Weymouth. He consulted the fireman and they both decided that it would be better to jump off since a crash seemed inevitable – there were no brakes.

They had no way of telling the guard at the back of the train, and he was astonished to see the crew standing by the track as the train rolled past – so he jumped off too.

The train entered Weymouth Station at speed, crashed through the station buildings and across the street before the engine turned over. The bang was heard for miles. Nobody was charged with any offence.

An engine driver in the 1850s.

25. The Demon Drink

The association between alcohol and crime is not confined to modern times. The ill-effects of over-consumption were always evident – not least the tendency to violence – but it was not until the sixteenth century that government became sufficiently worried by social disorder to attempt regulation. That regulation produced records which at least from the early seventeenth century give us some idea of drinking habits and consequences four hundred years ago.

The government was concerned with Keeping the Peace: and that included not only clamping down on bar-room brawls but eradicating dens of thieves or nests of potential rebellion. The traditional English alehouse was all too likely to arouse suspicion as a source of trouble, and so the first Licensing laws were passed by Parliament in 1552. From then until 2005 control of alehouses, inns and taverns – licensed premises – was vested in the Justices of the Peace. As it happened, it was in the sixteenth century that the increasing use of hops in the brewing process led to the greater strength of the drink, now known as beer.

Tipplers (sellers of ale and beer) applied annually to a magistrate who would take a recognisance from the applicant in the sum of £10, backed by further recognizances of £5 each from two other supporters. Misbehaviour meant forfeiture of the money and 'suppression' – ie the closure of the business.

Robert Hooper and Jane Puncknoll were keeping disorderly alehouses in Broadwey near Weymouth in September 1625. Dorset Quarter Sessions ordered that they were to be suppressed, arrested, and to give sureties that they would not sell ale again for three years: they were to be gaoled until the sureties were given. Seven tipplers of Sherborne were convicted of selling ale without licence in July 1636: they were each fined 20 shillings, and if they could not pay they were to be whipped. Three others were to be detained in the House of Correction for one month. In January 1629 at Blandford it was complained that Widow Gaye of Wimborne Minster *'doth brewe great quantities of of Beere or Ale in a Flewe or Chimney made of timber, to the great danger of the whole towne.'* The house actually caught fire during the holding of the Sessions. Her alehouse was suppressed and she was forbidden to continue brewing until the house was made suitable.

The Town Council in Dorchester briefly exerted further control in the 1630s when they initiated a municipal brewery, thereby controlling the strength of the beer and funding a number of social projects such as almshouses and an orphanage. At the time the governing middle-class was very Puritan, inspired by a charismatic Rector of Dorchester John White.

Licensing seems to have been rather lax in the early eighteenth century, but increasing concern about the consumption of spirits, especially gin, resulted in attempts by Parliament to tighten up. From 1753 candidates for a licence had to have a certificate from a local parson and from substantial local householders, that they were *"of good fame and of sober life and conversation."* In order that there should be closer control, the justices of each division were to hold annual 'Brewster Sessions' each September, when licences for the year would be considered.

Alehouses continued to grow in number and towards the end of the eighteenth century the feeling grew among more educated people that consumption of alcohol was related to poverty and crime. In 1787 the King issued a *Royal Proclamation against Vice and Immorality,* which was duly noticed in Dorset Quarter Sessions, and a stricter attitude was taken in licensing. This approach did not last long. It proved to be extremely unpopular throughout the country and justices were accused of favouring premises owned by brewers against the independent alehouse. The dislike of restriction grew apace, in line with the general economic attitude that freedom of trade even in alcohol would find the best solution. In 1830 an Act of Parliament took away almost all the licensing powers of magistrates, and allowed any ratepayer to open a shop for the sale of beer on payment of two guineas. Justices could order closure in case of riot. Only if the beershop owner also sold spirits did justices still have some general

Harvesting gang at Monkton – with flagons of cider.

control, so it was not unknown for magistrates to try to persuade alehousekeepers to take on the sale of gin as well!

From time to time local justices attempted to refuse licences where the sale of spirits allowed it, but appeals to Quarter Sessions were usually successful when lawyers were able to squeeze the letter of the law. For example, in September 1858, Robert Smith of the Three Mariners in Dorchester appealed against the refusal of the Dorchester Borough justices William Manfield (the Mayor) and John Ensor to grant him a licence. The appeal was allowed and damages and costs of £11 10s 8d awarded against the justices, though these were paid from county funds.

In 1868 Daniel Board, a licensee in Charmouth, appealed against a fine of £5.00 and costs for allowing noisy behaviour on his premises. The conviction was quashed and the costs of £28 12s 5d allowed against the justices – again paid from county funds.

It was not until 1869 and the years following that the powers of justices in licensing the sale of alcohol were re-established and remained in a similar form until 2005, when Licensing was transferred to Local Government. In 1872 Dorset Quarter Sessions registered its approval of the Wine and Beer Acts and hoped that they would continue. Under the Act of that year the Dorset Licensing Committee was set up, consisting of ten justices representative of the various divisions, to be reappointed annually. In 1874 Quarter Sessions approved detailed rules for the operation of the Licensing Committee: with the interests of the brewers, the licensees and the consumers and the well-being of the community all to be considered, the committee was working in a very sensitive area. Beer shops were encouraged to become Public Houses, licensed by the Justices. The familiar Dorset pub is usually well-administered and not a den of crime or insurrection, though town centres will have their problems associated with The Demon Drink.

THE TWENTIETH CENTURY

Across the country, recorded crime increased slowly from the 1870s, stabilised before World War One, resumed its increase slowly between the wars and then shot up in the last half of the twentieth century. Dorset followed this national pattern, but at a very low level.

The nature of crime, and society's attitudes to the different kinds of crime, also changed. With a rising standard of living for many, people possessed more things that were worth stealing, so burglary increased. On the other hand, drunkenness in public decreased as licensing laws were more strictly enforced. Casual violence became less tolerated and more likely to be prosecuted, and it too diminished. The huge advance in technology led to new kinds of crime, particularly associated with the motor-car and latterly with computers.

The crime of most interest to the general public is murder. Homicide is often casual and much more likely to be in the family than in the commission of another crime. Dorset's murder rate is in single figures in most years, and has varied very little since records began. Inevitably, murder makes the headlines!

26. The Tranquil 1930s

In the second half of the twentieth century it was not unusual for the elderly to look back to the years before World War Two with nostalgia for peaceful and orderly times. The war and its aftermath created such mayhem and upset and an apparent legacy of violence in society that the preceding decade acquired a golden glow of calm.

It is true that the prison population had been much lower in the 1930s, when petty offences attracted fewer prison sentences than before the Great War. Nevertheless, casual violence and petty thievery among the poorer classes continued largely unnoticed by the authorities and by the better-off.

The Second World War thrust people together in mutual distress, and with better education and communication (especially television) after the war, the living conditions and habits of all people became better known to all, and tolerance of bad behaviour diminished. More rigorous enforcement of the law followed, and the prison population inevitably rose. The popular press made the most of every opportunity to publicise crime, especially violence, and the impression grew that Britain – even Dorset – was hovering on the brink of anarchy. Recorded crime certainly mounted, but as always the actual extent of crime is unknown, and more effective policing and detection may have been partly responsible. In the early years of the twenty-first century recorded crime has gone down, though this fact has not received the same publicity. So why in the 1930s did a spate of murders in Dorset attract national attention?

In fact the records show that there was no great surge of homicides in the county during the decade, but it happened that there were some 'interesting' ones.

Alma Rattenbury.

Francis Rattenbury.

Frank Burdett

In 1930 'Captain' Frank Burdett was a talented leather craftsman working in Wimborne, who was given to boasting and lying when in drink. He was banned from his local, but was befriended by a farmer, Thomas Holloway. Burdett repaid the farmer's hospitality by courting his daughter Trixie, though he was at least three times her age. The Holloways did not approve, and forbade the match, but Trixie defied her parents and went to live with Burdett. At this period such an arrangement was disgraceful, and reluctantly the Holloways gave permission and the couple were married at the Register Office, though no member of the family was present.

Burdett was already in financial trouble, and asked his father-in-law for a loan, which was refused. Later he managed to persuade the farmer's wife to give him £18. This was soon spent and Burdett, now clearly deranged, borrowed a shotgun from an acquaintance 'to do some hunting'. Consumed with resentment he went to the farm early in the morning and shot both the Holloways in their bedroom. He shouted his determination to kill Trixie's four brothers as well, but they escaped from the house and raised the alarm. The police arrived to find the Holloways dead and the gunman gone. They began to search the area and soon found Burdett in Muddy Lane. He had shot himself but was still alive and died later.

As might be imagined, Trixie was distraught: her husband had murdered her parents and had killed himself. It was the stuff of tragic opera.

Alma Rattenbury and George Stoner

In 1935 Mr and Mrs Francis Rattenbury were living with their six-year-old son in their large and comfortable house in Bournemouth. They employed a housekeeper and a handyman chauffeur, and seemed to be happy enough. Actually, Alma Rattenbury was not so cheerful. At thirty-eight, she felt shackled to a very elderly man, and looked elsewhere for consolation. Fate delivered her a 'toy-boy' in the shape of eighteen-year-old George Stoner who had taken the job of handyman /chauffeur. He looked older, and had indeed given his age as twenty-two, but was quite naiive. He soon acquired a room in the house, and he and Alma became lovers. Mr Rattenbury seems not to have noticed, or possibly did not care.

On Sunday evening 24 March 1935 Alma played cards with her husband, retired to her own room and was joined by chauffeur George. George appeared agitated, and eventually admitted he had attacked her husband Francis, from motives which amounted to pure jealousy. Alma found Francis downstairs, very badly gashed about the head and bleeding copiously.

The doctor was called, and for better examination Francis was taken to a local Nursing Home. In view of the injuries, the police were summoned, but Alma was drinking large quantities of whisky and was soon incapable of answering questions. The following morning she made a statement saying she had hit Francis with a mallet at his own request as he was so depressed. Alma was arrested and duly charged. Francis died two days later and the charge became murder.

Meanwhile George Stoner had confessed to the murder privately to the housekeeper. She told the doctor who informed the police and George was arrested too.

George Stoner.

In due course both defendants were tried together at the Old Bailey, and both pleaded Not Guilty. By this time Alma had decided to give evidence against George. The trial lasted five days, and turned on whether the defendants had colluded in the murder. Alma was found Not Guilty, but George was sentenced to death.

While George awaited execution, Alma went to the banks of the River Avon near Christchurch, stabbed herself six times in the chest and fell in to the water.

George heard of her death, and in his Appeal pleaded his innocence and said he was now free to say that he had taken the blame to save Alma. The Appeal was rejected, but the death sentence was commuted to life imprisonment. He was released seven years later, and fought on D-Day in June 1944. He died in 2000.

Charlotte Bryant

In the early 1920s the British Army in Ireland was attempting to maintain order. A military policeman called Frederick Bryant met an Irish girl Charlotte

Charlotte Bryant.

McHugh and when he left the army he brought her back to his home county of Dorset. They married in 1922 and he worked as a cowman on a farm near Sherborne, and they lived in a poor cottage at Nether Compton.

If Charlotte had ever dreamt of a better life in England, she was quickly disillusioned: a cowman earned less than two pounds a week, and life was hard. Charlotte seems to have taken to going to the pub for consolation, and brought men home to add to her income. Frederick seems to have made no objection. Children were born, and in 1933 Charlotte developed a strong attachment to an itinerant horse-dealer called Leonard Parsons. Parsons lodged in the cottage, and he and Bryant became friends.

In 1935 Bryant suffered a series of severe stomach upsets. In October they moved to another cottage in Coombe near Bradford Abbas, but in November Parsons left, having apparently tired of his association with Charlotte. Charlotte made further efforts to make him return, but in vain.

In mid-December Frederick Bryant again fell seriously ill, and died just before Christmas. The doctors suspected poisoning with arsenic, and the post-mortem confirmed that this was the cause of death. Circumstantial evidence suggested strongly that Charlotte had bought arsenic, though this was never proved. There were indications in the boiler ashes that arsenic had been burnt there. Charlotte was duly charged with murder.

At the trial in Dorchester in May 1936 various witnesses gave their circumstantial evidence, and the jury found Charlotte guilty. Her appeal was rejected, and she was executed at Exeter in July. She made a will, leaving her total wealth of 5 shillings and a few coppers to be divided among her five children, who were taken in to care.

Women who murdered husbands especially with poison were always treated harshly: Charlotte Bryant may be compared with Mary Channing, burnt in 1705 at Maumbury Rings: and with Martha Brown publicly hanged on the Dorchester Prison gate in 1856.

Joseph Williams

In the crisis–ridden summer of 1939, with another Great War looming, an elderly Poole businessman had a personal trauma to face. Joseph Williams, a seventy-year-old retired army officer, had failed in business, had marital problems and was facing eviction from his house. Living in a single room, he went to see an old friend Walter Dinnivan to try to borrow money, as he had on previous occasions. He succeeded in getting only £5.

Dinnivan was well-off, having made money in the motor business, and had invested in property. His wife and son had died in the past year, and he lived with his grand-daughter. His grandson who was in the Royal Navy visited them on 20 May 1939, and the two young people went out to a dance. When they came back, Walter Dinnevan was lying on the floor dying from severe headwounds, and money and valuables had been taken.

The police cast a wide net for suspects and eventually landed on Joseph Williams. There appeared to be an obvious motive for robbery in Williams' dire circumstances, and a number of small pieces of evidence seemed to point directly to his involvement.

At the trial the Prosecution submitted these various pieces of evidence: Williams' thumb-print on a beer-glass found at the scene, saliva on cigarette-butts attributable to Williams' very rare blood-group, a blood-stained paper-bag of a kind of which a number were found in the defendant's room. But, as the Defence and later the judge pointed out, each of these pieces of evidence was explicable. The weapon was never found.

Williams was found Not Guilty. A reporter from the *News of the World* secured an exclusive interview, in which Williams maintained his innocence, but later that night confessed his guilt in confidence. In any case, under English law he could not have been retried for the same offence. The reporter held on to his secret until Williams died twelve years later in 1951, but was then able to use his 'scoop'.

27. Wartime Murder

A young soldier who had survived the escape of the British Expeditionary Force at Dunkirk in the summer of 1940 was hanged for murder in Dorchester just over a year later.

Private David Jennings, stationed in Dorchester Barracks, had received a rejection letter from his girlfriend. Apparently on Sunday 26 January he decided to drown his sorrows with his comrades, and drank heavily at the 'George', the 'Antelope' and the 'Ship'. He bought several rounds of drinks, and probably used the money he had been saving for his wedding. Back in the barracks the drunken Jennings changed into his working battledress, took his rifle and some ammunition, and went back into the town. After an unsuccessful attempt to shoot off the lock on an office safe in Princes Street, the NAAFI Canteen (a café for servicemen) seemed to promise some restoration of his finances, and he broke in. Frustrated by a locked door, he fired his rifle six times. One of those shots killed the nightwatchman. Back in the barracks he admitted what he had done, and was arrested.

The immediate issue for the prosecution was – murder or manslaughter? Had Jennings fired at the man intentionally? The charge of murder was proffered, and in June the trial took place at the Assizes in the building now known as the Old Crown Court. The jury found the defendant guilty, sentence of death was pronounced, and the appeal to the Court of Appeal was rejected. Petitions for clemency from Jennings' home town of Warrington and from the MP form West Dorset were rejected by the Home Secretary, and on 23 July 1941 David Jennings became the last person to be hanged in Dorchester Prison.

28. The Portland Spy Ring

In the years following World War Two there developed a growing mutual antipathy between the nations of the West and the Soviet Union. In this 'Cold War' the former allies were deeply suspicious of each other's motives and intentions, and spying on both sides became a huge issue. Some spies were the employed agents of their own governments, and some were individuals who had become convinced of the rightness of the cause opposed to their own. As always, there were those who sold the secret material to which they had access for the immediate monetary reward: the so-called 'Portland Spy Ring' came into this category.

Harry Houghton, having served in the Royal Navy during the war, had worked in the British Embassy in Poland as a clerk in the early 1950s. Some nefarious dealings there led to a connection which was developed when Houghton was later employed at the Admiralty Underwater Weapons Establishment on Portland. He was sought out by a Russian secret service officer who posed as an American naval commander wanting to check what the British were doing with secret information passed to them from the USA. The agent used the name Gordon Lonsdale, and in due course substantial material collected by Houghton was given to him in return for money.

A filing-clerk at AUWE called Ethel Gee was drawn into the plot when she and Houghton became lovers in 1958. She was able to take interesting files for Houghton to photograph and return. At one point the couple were making regular weekend trips to London to exchange packets with Lonsdale on Waterloo Station.

The extra money enabled a more extravagant lifestyle for both, and their frequent drinking sessions at the Elm Tree Inn at Langton Herring occasioned

The Elm Tree Inn.

comment; to this day the oak corner-settle in the pub is pointed out as their particular nook. Information was given to the police who notified Special Branch, and a watch was kept.

In January 1961 the Waterloo trip was followed, and Lonsdale was observed taking the packet to an address in Ruislip. This was the home of Mr and Mrs Kroger who were antiquarian booksellers, but were also Soviet agents who sent the information to Moscow by inscribing ancient tomes with microdots and posting them. All five of the ring were arrested, tried and sent to prison. Later the Russians were exchanged for captured British spies, but Houghton and Gee each served nine years of a fifteen-year sentence. After release in 1970 they were married.

PART TWO

WHAT WORKS?

Throughout history society has sought ways to maintain the peace, to establish rules for communal living and to enforce those rules. The aim of Criminal Justice is to reduce crime. The very nature of humanity means that the system can never be more than partially successful, and the extent of that success can only be estimated. In the past hundred years enormous efforts have been expended in searching for 'What Works'.

In the United Kingdom the succession of Criminal Justice Acts of Parliament bears witness to the government's determination to get to grips with the complexities of human behaviour in an age of soaring material standards, rapid economic change and multicultural society. The cost of those efforts as a proportion of national income has ballooned – but in the first decades of the twenty-first century there is satisfaction that the crime rate overall is lessening. The problem now is to find out why.

Plaque in Wareham Magistrates' Court.

'What Works?' is the question that dominates criminology. Deterrence, retribution, diversion, education, rehabilitation have all played their part and as answers all have their supporters, but the magic recipe is far from established. For most of the past thousand years deterrence has dominated, but society has rejected its extreme forms, and there is much evidence to show that it is not very effective – but then that is true of the other disposals also.

As this section demonstrates, Dorset has been the scene for a wide variety of attempts to deter or reform, and the search goes on.

29. Pains and Penalties

Capital Punishment

From the twelfth century through to the eighteenth century all crimes recognised as Grand Felonies were punishable by death.

Grand Felonies included theft of goods worth 12 pence or more, murder, treason, forgery and many others. The list greatly increased during eighteenth century, as Parliament acceded to the fears of the landed classes, and by 1800 there were more than two hundred capital offences. Many death sentences were not carried out, but commuted to transportation to the colonies which became available from 1598 – though little used until the colonies developed on the east coast of America and in the West Indies.

Execution was normally carried out by hanging in public on gallows in Dorchester. For many years the place of execution was at the top of what is now called Icen Way and the site is marked by the statues of the Roman Catholic martyrs of the sixteenth and early seventeenth centuries. Subsequently a gallows was erected near Maumbury Rings which provided a convenient viewpoint for the onlookers. After the new prison was built in 1795 just behind North Square the top of the gatehouse was used, and the crowds could gather in the fields across the river for a good view. Executions ceased to be public in the 1860s, and were carried out in a purpose-built 'topping-shed' within the prison. The last person hanged in Dorchester seems to have been a soldier convicted of murder in 1941 (see page 82).

In the seventeenth and eighteenth centuries executions usually followed the Assizes held in March and July, when people suspected of capital crimes were

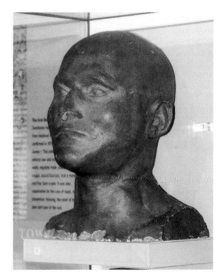

Plaster cast of murderer hanged at Dorchester in 1869.

The gallows, the pillory, and whipping at the cart's tail..

tried before the visiting judge and a local jury. Records are sparse, but it seems that often the tally of executions reached only two or three and in some cases there were none.

The dramatic reduction from the 1830s in the list of crimes punishable by death meant even fewer executions, and much more ghoulish interest in those that were carried out. Some greater sense of compassion is evidenced in the use of 'mercy weights', which were attached to the legs of the victim to increase the tightening of the noose and thereby speed up strangulation. These weights are now displayed in the Dorset County Museum. Further such niceties included the use of the 'New Drop' on the prison gate which helped with the same effect and eventually resulted in the scientific breaking of the neck and thereby instant loss of consciousness and subsequent death.

A further sophistication in the infliction of the death penalty was the extra pain for treason. Hanging drawing and quartering was regarded as the ultimate deterrent for potential traitors, and was most famously applied across Dorset as punishment in the Monmouth Rebellion of 1685. This could be used in so-called petty treason by men who murdered their masters. Wives who murdered their husbands were like wise guilty of petty treason, and the punishment was to be burnt at the stake. The best known example is that of Mary Channing, who was executed at Maumbury Rings in 1705 for poisoning her husband, though the executioner kindly strangled her first before lighting the pyre.

First offenders could sometimes escape the death penalty by pleading 'benefit of clergy'. This is explained more fully on page 121.

A pillory in action.

In the reforming nineteenth century this anomaly was abolished. By the early seventeenth century Grand Felony was mainly left to the judge at the Assizes, though a few felons were executed in Dorset after sentence by magistrates at Quarter Sessions.

Nicholas Grant stole six sheep and was hanged in April 1635. In September the same year Elizabeth Johnson alias Stevens was declared to be an *'incorrigible vagabond'*, sentenced to death and duly hanged. In the record, the execution is indicated by the clerk with the note 'sus' against her name – abbreviated Latin for *'suspensus :* suspended or hanged.

The full rigour of the law in respect of potentially-capital offences was pursued only in a minority of cases, thus making justice a lottery and weakening whatever deterrent value the death-penalty might have had. Death was felt by many people to be too harsh for most first offences, moderate thefts, or

Opposite: Execution site at top of Icen Way, Dorchester.

Plounsing, a traditional penalty for female scolds and slanderers. Sometimes postponed 'until the weather be warmer…'

Eighteenth-century execution.

trespasses. Devices in the system for avoiding it included under-valuing stolen goods, benefit of clergy and refusals of juries to convict.

There are occasional references to the costs of burying those who had been executed under sentence from the Assizes, and in September 1793 it was ordered that

'the Western Treasurer do pay unto Messrs Gritton and Lake Carpenters etc the sum of Sixteen Shillings being the Contents of their Bill now delivered into this Court for Carpenters Work done and Materials used for the said County in repairing and amending the Gallows at Forthington Down.'

The gallows were repaired again by the same firm at Easter 1795. Later on executions were carried out on the roof of the prison gatehouse and in the summer of 1864 it was suggested in Quarter Sessions that the High Sheriff should be paid £10 *'for his extra expenses in effecting the execution of the criminal Preedy'.*

Corporal Punishment

Petty felony was punishable by whipping or branding – or both – or by a fine. In January 1630 Edith, wife of Roger Freeman, was sentenced to be branded on the left hand with the letter T (for Thief), whipped through the town of Blandford and released. Other letters could be used: R for Rogue, V for Vagabond. Branding could be on the thumb, the cheek or the shoulder, and would be a permanent disfigurement. Bartholomew Forde, Anthony Dunford and Englishe Tucker read and were sentenced to be branded at Blandford Sessions in 1626, but we do not know their crimes.

Violence was so common in everyday life in most periods in history that unless it resulted in loss of life or limb it was unlikely to attract severe punishment. Assault and affray were almost always dealt with by heavy fines varying from the equivalent of two weeks' income for a working man, 3 shillings and 4 pence, to 20 shillings for a gentleman who assaulted another man's wife.

Forgery and deceit were treated very seriously, and the pillory was often used in punishment. It might not seem that to stand for an hour locked in a wooden frame, even on successive market days, was such a heavy penalty. In fact, it could be very severe, since being pelted with whatever the crowd thought suitable could result in injury and even death.

Gregory Hillary was sentenced at Sherborne in 1634

'To be whipt att the foot of the pillory on the next market day in this Towne – then to stand on the pillory immediately after by the space of 2 houres with an Inscription "For gaining money by false messages." After that to be openly whipt on the next market day at Dorchester and to stand 2 houres more in the pillory there with the same inscription. Then to remayne in the house of Correction for six monethes, and from thence until he finde good suertyes for his good behaviour.'

The lesser penalty of six hours in the stocks was applied in petty felony as an alternative to whipping. It was uncomfortable and possibly embarrassing, as the victim sat locked in by his ankles and possibly wrists, though it was not as

Eighteenth-century magistrates court.

dangerous as the pillory. Nor did the stocks provide so much public entertainment, as is shown in the illustration by W. S. Pyne on page 89.

Magistrates, looking to deter further petty crime in the miscreant and others, frequently chose whipping, either private or public. The severity of the punishment must have been variable, but this seems to have been left to the official carrying it out. In June 1635 Mary Flemming was convicted at Shaftesbury of stealing half a measure of barley worth four pence and sentenced to be whipped and released.

Until the nineteenth century public whipping was seen as an appropriate punishment for minor offences committed by lower-class people of both sexes. It fulfilled the most basic popular demand – it was deterrent (apparently), it was retributive, it was spectacular, it was cheap: and unlike hanging, if a mistake was made, well, no great harm was done, since all children and many women and servants were frequently lashed anyway.

Village stocks.

Acts of Parliament establishing corporal punishment for offences sometimes gave specific instructions as to how it was to be carried out. The market-place on market day was mentioned, sometimes through the town, sometimes a number of consecutive occasions for the one offence, sometimes at the beginning and end of a prison sentence. Usually the offender was to be stripped to the waist and whipped *'until his or her body be bloody'*. Curiously the instrument to be used was not indicated, but from contemporary drawings it seems likely that it was usually a bundle of birch twigs, though something like a 'cat of nine tails' (strings of twine or leather attached to a handle) may have been used. The offender could be tied to a permanent whipping post, or if he (or she) was to be whipped through the town he could be tied to the tail of a cart.

Successive generations in some families seem to have suffered thus: at Bridport in 1664 Frances Rider was sentenced *'to be whipped till her body bleed'* for vagrancy and sixty years later Thomas Rider was whipped in the same town and then sent to the House of Correction for twelve months. In the summer of 1754 at Shaftesbury whipping appears to have been in fashion: one man was whipped in both Shaftesbury and Sherborne, another was whipped privately and five men were whipped and discharged from the House of Correction. The following October only one prisoner was in the gaol awaiting trial. Catherine Brown's victim was paid £1 8s for prosecuting her and had the satisfaction of seeing her whipped and sent to the House of Correction for six months.

Towards the end of the eighteenth century sentences of whipping by Quarter Sessions diminished, but occasionally there was a return to tried and trusted methods, as in 1819 when six men were imprisoned for one year with hard labour, at the end of which they were to be publicly and severely whipped – Samuel Mates at Bere Regis, William Miller at Weymouth, James New the Younger at Mappowder, William Morgan at Handley, William West at Blandford and Thomas Read at Cranborne. These must have been among the last public whippings: women were not whipped at all after 1820, but men continued to suffer private whippings until 1861.

The Old Crown Court in Dorchester.

In September 1845 Elisha Wilmot who had pleaded guilty was sentenced to eighteen months' hard labour and to be twice privately whipped, and several other whippings were ordered by the same court. The last adult male to be whipped by Dorset Quarter Sessions was Samuel Gillett in January 1859, who was described as an incorrigible rogue and vagabond and also received three months' imprisonment. Whipping of boys with a birch rod and a specified number of strokes continued. This was usually a sentence following conviction in Petty Sessions or by two magistrates, but sometimes in Quarter Sessions as when Robert Ridout was given fourteen days' hard labour and six strokes of the birch for larceny in October 1873.

Fines

With no police force, the maintenance of regulations depended heavily on the reporting of offences by aggrieved citizens. The reward for such reporting and giving of evidence in prosecution was the payment of half the fine imposed. The result was the existence of a band of professional informers, who produced lists of offenders at each Quarter Sessions. The relationship between magistrates and informers was rather prickly: it is clear that the justices did not always trust the evidence brought and when an informer was caught out in corrupt practice he was heavily punished.

Frequently offenders prosecuted for trading matters would ask to discuss and compound with the informer, which meant that they would pay him a smaller sum in return for his withdrawing the prosecution. The court was glad to accede to this as it saved valuable time – though the king did not get his share of the money.

The breaking of trade regulations was meat and drink to the informers, who could obtain a steady income from their share of the fines. What might pass for clever business today was a misdemeanour and punishable in the seventeenth century. Selling at a profit without adding to the value of goods, engrossing or buying large quantities in order to profit in scarcity and trading outside the market place and given times, were all subject to prosecution.

A 'Not Guilty' plea to a misdemeanour was tried by a process known as 'traverse', and the defendant was entitled to use counsel – at his own expense. While felonies were usually tried at the Sessions where the charge was made, traverse trials were often respited or adjourned to the next Sessions.

In both felonies and misdemeanours, juries were impanelled to hear the evidence and deliver verdicts. After the imposition of a fine, the offender was committed to gaol until the fine was paid to the sheriff. Such a process today might have a remarkable effect on the fine-recovery rate!

30. Dorchester Prison

There was a prison in Dorchester for seven hundred years. For the last two centuries it was on its present site: grim, forbidding and stark, but out of sight for most of the town.

In 1305 King Edward I granted the right for the commonalty of Dorchester to make their own prison, and a gaoler was appointed. The 'Prison' seems to have been one room in the gaoler's house, which may have been on the corner of Cornhill and High East Street. Since no records survive before the seventeenth century, we can only surmise that there were not many inmates. A prison was merely a secure place in which accused persons could be kept until trial: imprisonment as a punishment was rare, the assumption being that retribution would be physical or financial. Petty crime was dealt with promptly by magistrates. More serious cases would await the arrival of a royal judge on his circuit for Gaol Delivery and Assizes.

The Quarter Sessions Order Book beginning in 1625 provides the earliest record of the business of the county magistrates and gives useful evidence of part played by Dorchester Prison at that time. The Justices of the Peace or magistrates had been maintaining law and order since 1361, but under the Tudor monarchs their functions and powers had been immensely increased, and by the early seventeenth century the JPs were effectively the county council as well as the local judiciary. They administered the prison, and collected a rate from county ratepayers to fund it.

King George III visiting prisoners in Dorchester.

The outer gate of Dorchester Prison in North Square – late nineteenth century.

The Seventeenth Century Prison

Recently a purpose-built gaol had been created at the bottom of High East Street, near the River Frome: not an ideal site since it was liable to flood. Part of the building was used as the 'House of Correction', an institution which was authorised under the Elizabethan Poor Law for the punishment of idle rogues and vagabonds.

In effect the House of Correction was more like the later conception of 'prison', in that incarceration was a penalty imposed by the court. Other towns in the county attempted to create Houses of Correction, and for a while the Sherborne

Plan for Dorchester Prison, 1795.

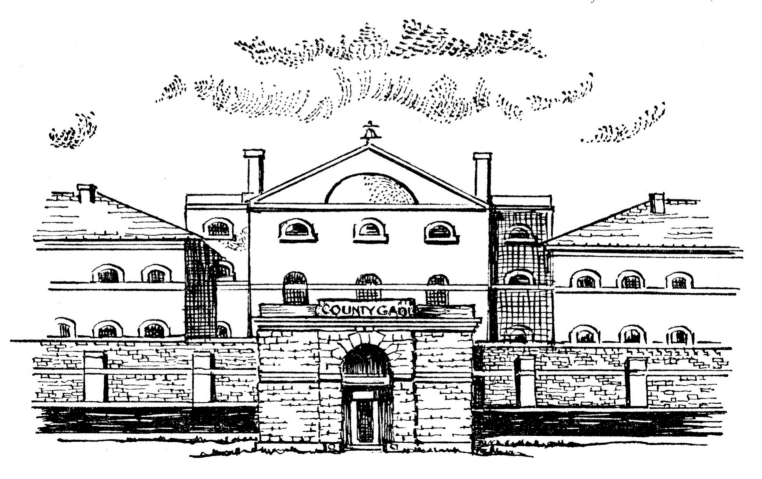

house was regarded by the justices as replacing the one in Dorchester – but the Dorchester house was re-established.

Thomas Devenish

From 1627 until 1638 Thomas Devenish was the Keeper of the Gaol and the Master of the House of Correction. A committee of four justices led by Sir Francis Ashley was set up to supervise the prison and in particular to determine what fees the prisoners should pay the keeper. The system was that only a prisoner without other means was entitled to a bread allowance and everybody else negotiated a board-and-lodging rate with the keeper.

The county sheriff also had rights in the prison, including the right to hold people in custody while bail was being arranged. It became an issue between the keeper and the sheriff in 1632 and Devenish lost. This meant that his annual stipend was reduced from £40 to £20 per year.

A year later a concern arose over a cottage and ground next door to the prison. It seemed that the ground would be suitable for the exercising of the prisoners – giving them an *'ayringe'*. The property was bought from the executors of the owner, and the cottage made over for the use of the keeper – now often called the governor or gaoler.

Devenish believed in 'setting the poore on work' and drew substantial sums of money from the magistrates for tools in 1631 and more again for a handmill for grinding malt in 1632. He presented another detailed bill in 1635, for a sackcloth loom, stocks to beat hemp, iron combs, spinning wheels and heavy hammers.

This might seem to show that Devenish was doing exactly what was required of him – training inmates of the Gaol and House of Correction in habits of industry. Perhaps he was, but by April 1637 dissatisfaction was recorded with the way in which the gaol was being run, and in October it was said that Devenish was using the grounds for his own benefit, and not *'airing and refreshing the prisoners'*.

Calendar of the House of Correction
January 1629 – with transcription.

Kalender del domo Dorrecois

Calendar of the House of Correction

Rose Lane	to remain in the House of Correction until the next Sessions; the parish of Ryme Intrinseca to provide her with clothes.
Grace Spinny	to remain there for one year.
John Bent	to remain there until the next Sessions.
Wilmot Curteis	discharged, and ordered to get a master within one month or be sent back.
Othaniell Saunders	discharged upon trial.
Christian Slade	discharged.
Ralph Samwayes	to remain there until discharged by Roger Gollop, esquire.
George Wootton } Christian Seamour	to be well whipped, released, 'and sent by passe from Tythinge to Tythinge (beinge very dangerous persons) unto the Cittye of Exon.'

1784 'The House that Jack Built…'
The first new prison in Dorchester
was the subject of satirical verse.

At the Assizes held at Blandford in July the judge had ordered the magistrates to investigate abuses said to have been committed by Devenish, and as a result he was dismissed at the October Sessions. Early in 1638 it was agreed that a new set of orders would be drawn up for the conduct of the prison.

The new rules duly appeared and were recorded in the Order Book.

The New Regime

The rooms used for the House of Correction were now to be workrooms where any of the inmates including debtors and felons would be paid for their work at the rate of four pence per day. Women and juveniles over fourteen were to receive three pence a day. The sheriff was to appoint the gaoler and would have the right to imprison during his year of office. One penny a day per prisoner would be allowed to feed bread to poor prisoners – others must pay. The gaoler was not to brew beer for sale to prisoners, but must buy it in the town for sale at one penny a quart. The gaoler could charge fourteen pence a week for room-rent to be paid by prisoners who could afford it, but only six pence in the communal room. The gaoler was to read a chapter of the Bible to the assembled prisoners twice a day. There were to be no social gatherings with non-inmates at the gaol. Prisoners revealing plots to escape were to be rewarded. The prison was to be kept clean and well-maintained. The County Treasurers were to supervise the gaol and inspect it at least four times a year.

Later the House of Correction was reinstated following urgent demands from Judges sitting in Assize, but the office of Master of the House of Correction was separated from the office of gaoler – Thomas Devenish had wielded too much power!

The County Gaol remained at the foot of High East Street in Dorchester until the 1780s. The building must have been small and insanitary, but it was not expected that inmates would be there long. There are no surviving records from 1638 until 1663, probably because of the chaos of the Civil War and the period of the Cromwellian republic, but in the 1660s some attempts were made to improve

Dorchester Gaol Calendar
1635

Elizabeth Johnson *alias* Stevens	as vagrant and incorrigible vagabond, to be hanged. *Hanged*.
Stephen Whittmore Nicholas Lee Bridget Palmer Mary Freind	as vagrants and dangerous rogues, to be branded on the left shoulder with the letter R and sent by pass to their birthplaces.
Basil Tanner, wife of Robert	for stealing 16 bundles of linen thread worth 10d, to be whipped and released.
Robert Hardey	for stealing a wether sheep worth 11d, to be whipped and released.
Robert Coxe	for stealing 15 knots of linen thread worth 10d, to be whipped and released.
Robert Sampson	for stealing one bundle of barley worth 6d, to be whipped and released.
William Palmer	for vagrancy, to be whipped and sent by pass to his birthplace.

conditions. New tiling cost £10, and a supply of fresh water from the River Frome was organised, with a channel and a series of hatches. Shortly afterwards Thomas Knapton the keeper reported that persons unknown had broken and cut the waterway. The sanitation system had been destroyed and there was *'excrement soaking through the wall'*. Perhaps the doubtful quality of the water played a part in the provision of a furnace for brewing small beer at a cost of £13 13s 8d in 1664.

The Georgian Gaol

Numbers in the gaol seldom went beyond a dozen and frequently there were fewer. In the quiet mid-eighteenth century it was often nearly empty – in March 1761 there was only one prisoner. The baker's bill for bread supplied to the poor prisoners was regularly presented to the magistrates at Quarter Sessions. The keeper made his profit from the fees paid for board and lodging by the better-off inmates. When he incurred extra expense, such as for medical care, the burial of prisoners dying in custody, or the conveying to Weymouth or Bristol of those sentenced to transportation, the keeper was reimbursed by the County Treasurer.

For many years in the mid-eighteenth century the gaol was run by the Chaffey family – first James and then his son Batt. The health of prisoners seems to have received more attention at this time: a gaol surgeon was appointed part-time in the 1770s. Sometimes medical care was rather amateur: during an outbreak of smallpox in 1785 Batt Chaffey *'inoculated Joseph Wellstead a Criminal in the natural way'*. Presumably the keeper had heard of the activities of Benjamin Jesty at Yetminster.

Although the gaolkeeper had always received an allowance, this was augmented by the fees paid by prisoners. Until 1774 even acquitted prisoners were required to pay a fee to the gaoler before they were released. It was felt necessary to pay the gaoler an extra £20 a year in 1784 because Parliament no longer allowed him to sell alcoholic liquor to the inmates!

A New Prison

The gaol at the foot of High East Street in Dorchester was rebuilt in 1784 (see page 103), but when the prison reformer John Howard visited in 1787 he was very critical: it was badly planned, the rooms were dirty and not whitewashed, and the bread was of poor quality. The magistrates appointed a new Gaol Committee, which recommended that all the gaoler's fees from the inmates should be abolished in return for a salary of £150 per year.

The general feeling was that only a larger prison on a bigger site could meet the increasing demand and the higher standards. The architect William Blackburn was asked to put forward ideas for a combined prison and House of Correction. The latter was sometimes called a 'Bridewell', after the London establishment of that

*House of Correction or
'Bridewell' (Hogarth).*

name. Blackburn attended the prison committee in November 1788. His plan was accepted and the site of Castle Hill at the top end of the town was chosen.

Tenders were invited and it was agreed to raise a subscription to find the estimated £10,000. One hundred and twenty-five subscribers, led by the vigorous William Morton Pitt lent the money at 4% and it was all repaid by 1807. In the event the gaol was built by John Fentiman and cost rather more than £13,000.

The new gaol was built in the early 1790s and not surprisingly took longer than expected. Its progress was carefully monitored by the committee. It consisted of a walled enclosure in which there was a centre block and four smaller blocks connected to the centre by iron bridges. A substantial entrance building formed part of the wall. The ground was divided into courtyards with separate access from the blocks, so it was possible to achieve the separation of different classes of inmate, which was one of the reforms urged by John Howard. With separate working rooms, male and female infirmaries, visiting rooms and single cells, it was a far cry from the old gaol with its open wards and casual mix.

Alterations began almost immediately and continued throughout the life of the building. In October 1797 Quarter Sessions resolved

'that the Door into the first Cell in the Females Bridewell be walled up, and a Wooden Door placed in the South Side of the said Cell to open into the Male Penitentiary Court'. It was further resolved that *'the Ventilating Holes in the backs of the Cells throughout the Gaol which only afford the means of intercourse and Communication between the several Classes of Prisoners and which are found by Experience to be perfectly unnecessary be stopped up.'*

The Flow of Reform

The traditional division between a prison for temporary detention and a house of correction for punishment, was now clearly at an end. Sentences of imprisonment were being used increasingly. The House of Correction (or Bridewell) at Sherborne was closed in 1793 and its function transferred to one of the wings of the new gaol. A copy of the regulations for the County Gaol in Gloucester, drawn up by the reformer Sir George Onesiphorous Paul, was obtained and some attempt made to follow their pattern in Dorchester. Under an Act of 1791 two justices had to be appointed as visitors to the gaol in each quarter.

The visiting justices were clearly dissatisfied in 1804, when serious charges were brought against the governor, George Andrews.

'First. That the said Gaoler did employ many of the Prisoners to work and labour in and about his private Concerns, contrary to the established Laws of this Realm, and contrary to the Sentences passed on them by the Judges etc, etc.

Second. That the said Gaoler did refuse to obey the standing Orders of the visiting Magistrates by admitting Prisoners sentenced to Confinement to be employed in and about his Dwelling-House as domestic Servants; by employing the said Prisoners to work for his Family, in their Apartments or Wards, after the usual Hours for being locked up; by suffering an illicit Intercourse between the Men Prisoners, and others, with the Women Prisoners, contrary to the Rules and fundamental Principles of the said Gaol; and also by making false Representations to the visiting Magistrates of the Situation of the Prison, Prisoners etc etc...'

The charges continue, and include ill-treatment of prisoners, the use of *'horrid Oaths and Imprecations'*, neglect of the sick, failure to keep the prison clean and downright corruption. Somehow the governor survived! Just as in the operation of the Poor Law, the idea that inmates should earn their keep and at the same time learn a useful trade, appealed to authorities and general public. Prisoners were employed during the building operation and later in timber-cutting, netting, tailoring and hatting. A hatting-shed was built, the money being raised by William Morton Pitt. The profits were divided between the county, the keeper and the prisoners according to their status.

The justices resolved that Mr Andrews (the governor) *'do purchase Linen to be made into Shirts and Shifts by the Female Prisoners for the use of the Prisoners in General'*. Numbers in the gaol fluctuated, with a high point of 126 being reached in 1816, at a time of post-war dislocation.

Hard Labour

The common sentence in the House of Correction had been to 'hard labour', from its origin as a means of training idle rogues in habits of industry. The need to provide some form of rigorous occupation led to enquiries being made in 1820 as to the merits of corn-mills established in other prisons. Sir William Cubitt, a civil engineer, had invented a 'treadmill' in 1818. This consisted of a large paddlewheel with twenty-four spokes. Convicts would step on to a paddle and climb, thus turning the wheel. The power developed by a squad of such men could be used to grind corn or for other purposes – though it could simply

Treadmill.

be used as a penal regime. It was calculated on an eight-hour shift an individual would have climbed the equivalent of 7200 feet – without going anywhere. The operation had three purposes: it was punitive, it tired the convicts so that they would be too exhausted to give trouble, and it might bring some profit if corn was actually ground.

In March 1821 Dorset Quarter Sessions ordered a treadmill, to be used for grinding corn, and shortly afterwards a similar machine was installed for women prisoners. The women's mill rapidly fell into disuse and was taken down and re-erected on the men's side. The justices laid down regulations for the periods of labour, with appropriate breaks according to season. Silence was imposed on the treadwheel.

Equipment, Discipline and Security

New furniture provided for the gaol in the 1790s included iron plank bedsteads, with debtors and those owing fines having beds with wooden laths and 6 inches wider than the rest. At a time when the heating of the courts was giving concern, it is interesting that in January 1831 the justices ordered that the galleries of the prison were to be warmed *'by Mr Price's Apparatus of warm water'*. Socialising in the gaol was not permitted – there was to be no communication between male and female prisoners. Quarter Sessions ordered that the gaoler was not to convey letters or parcels from one prisoner to another!

In 1809 chains were fixed across each cell door for extra security and an iron palisade was proposed in 1829 between the courts of the prison, instead of a wooden stockade, on the basis that this would make further measures to secure the outer wall unnecessary. Escapes were clearly in mind because a year later Quarter Sessions ordered that bells connected with wires should be placed on the walls.

Prison discipline became harsher. New rules drawn up in 1834 stated that convicted felons were to be kept separate at meal-times, silence was to be enforced among prisoners at all times and additional turnkeys were to be appointed to enforce the rule of silence. Prisoners were not to do their own cooking and a hard diet was set out: for example, prisoners under fourteen were to be given 1lb of bread per day, 1½ pints of oatmeal gruel for breakfast, 1½ lbs of potatoes with salt for dinner and a pint of gruel for supper.

Inspection

The Prisons Act of 1835 appointed inspectors to visit all local prisons; the inspectors were to require justices to maintain recommended standards. On paper it was revolutionary, subjecting the county to the authority of the Home Secretary and his staff – in practice the justices generally managed to carry on in the way they intended, which usually involved more concern with effects on rates than 'fanciful ideas' of central government. One of the fanciful ideas carried out was the installation of a bath in the female ward of the House of Correction in 1845. Even though the Bridewell had been absorbed within the prison fifty years earlier it was still referred to as the House of Correction. Another proposal was to light part of the gaol with gas though not, of course, the cells.

Occasional ripples disturbed the apparent calm surface of gaol life. In 1853 it was complained that the entrance to the gaol was inadequate and that people were throwing tobacco over the walls amongst the prisoners. In September 1860 there was a debate at Quarter Sessions concerning flogging as a punishment for indiscipline in the gaol.

It was emphasised that visiting justices could order floggings, but that a justice should be present, together with a surgeon who had the duty to reduce the punishment if necessary. One justice was sure that of late years punishments had been much milder than previously. The records suggest that such punishment was very rare. At this time there was an influx of 24 naval prisoners, whose conduct was noted to be very bad, but even their punishments were not corporal. In 1864 the Rev. C.W. Bingham, in presenting the report of the visiting justices, said that two boys had been given six strokes with a birch rod, but that they had laughed!

Value for Money?

Doubts as to the efficacy of imprisonment were raised by the chaplain in 1863 – *'The large number of re-committals to our prison shows how small is the deterring effect that confinement in it exercises upon the minds of the criminal classes.'* Rewards for good conduct were being made to discharged prisoners e.g. *'Henry Churchill, first sentence of 6 months - 10 shillings.'* In 1865 it was ordered that notices of discharge and behaviour should be sent to the clergymen of the prisoner's parish and the attention of Quarter Sessions was drawn to the *'Society to aid Discharged Prisoners not of the Worst Class '*. Presumably the 'Worst Class' were beyond redemption, and therefore undeserving of help with rehabilitation.

Concern about prisons in general had been growing, particularly in connection with the great variety of regimes across the country. In 1865 another Prison Act provided that central government money allowances might be withheld if the Home Office rules were not carried out. Three years later the Home Office decided to refuse the government allowance to Dorset because their inspector had pronounced the prison to be inefficient and had warned that the prison must be brought within the requirements of the Prison Act.

The Inspector of Prisons wrote to Quarter Sessions, objecting that prisoners had no lighting in the cells and therefore *'pass nearly 12 hours in bed at all seasons of the year'*. There were no bells or gongs in the cells for prisoners to communicate with the turnkeys. There were protests from the justices – *'We have as healthy a gaol as can be found in England'*. The inspector's criticism of the heating provoked indignation in the chairman of the visiting justices, Mr Foster – *'Our own servants at home do not have fires in their bedrooms, yet it is insisted upon that the cells should be warmed at night for the prisoners! (Laughter)'*.

The Government Takes Over

The loss of the allowance was serious, and negotiations with the Home Office continued. In 1870 the galleries to the cells were enclosed and the prison sewer was connected with the main sewer for Dorchester on the opposite side of the river, but relations with the Inspectorate were always difficult.   Mr Foster retired as chairman at Easter 1874, aged nearly eighty-eight. A couple of years later the government decided to take complete charge of all prisons. There was no great opposition to this: it seemed that the justices had had enough of the long struggle with Whitehall and in any case it meant that the whole cost was removed from the rates.

It was suggested that the county should be compensated for loss of property and the new chairman of the visitors Everard Hambro JP outlined the cost of the original building and of all the alterations, additions and improvements since, including the umbrella provided to protect the woman who opened the prison gate.

Everard Hambro JP.

Aerial view of Dorchester Prison taken in the 1960s and showing prisoners walking in the exercise yard.

Mr Hambro assessed the total at £81,608 18s lld. The Commissioners of Prisons reported that the *'prison was in every way unsuitable'* and it would be necessary to rebuild it. There was further indignation and Mr Hambro pointed out that this was considered to be the best gaol in England, but to no avail and the matter was allowed to subside.

Under the Prisons Act 1877 the justices continued to appoint a visiting committee. Their reports were frequently concerned with the failure of the Home Office to pay the pensions of retired prison staff at the level that the county would have paid.

In 1880 there was a strong protest about the state of discipline at the prison and there were complaints by the prisoners against the governor and chief warder. The committee protested that the Commissioners had not kept them informed of incidents at the prison and the chairman talked of 'Star Chamber government' – an echo of 250 years before!

Quarter Sessions continued to appoint justices to be members of the Visiting Committee to Dorchester Prison. Parallel to this work was the operation of the Board of Visitors to Portland Convict Prison. The Boards of Visitors to the convict prisons such as Dartmoor and Parkhurst were created by Act of Parliament in 1898.

Appointment to a Board of Visitors was made by the Home Office and since the demise of Quarter Sessions in 1973, all prisons have had Boards of Visitors, now called Independent Monitoring Boards. Many members of the boards are justices, but lay members play an important part. Inspections are carried out by rota, and reports made to regular meetings of the board, which itself presents an annual report to the Home Secretary.

Until the 1990s Boards of Visitors also acted in a judicial capacity, trying and punishing offenders against prison discipline. Punishments awarded included restricted diet, solitary confinement, loss of earnings, loss of remission and for the first half of the twentieth century, flogging with a cat-of-nine-tails.

Prison Staff

Over the whole period, from the seventeenth century onwards, the development of the prison was reflected in the status and responsibility of the staff.

Initially the keeper regarded the gaol as a family business, in which his salary was augmented by the fees payable by prisoners and by the charges he made for services and provisions. Successive members of the Chaffey family were the gaolkeepers from 1722 to 1786, the Andrews family from 1786 to 1843. Towards the end of the eighteenth century began the move towards the replacement of fees and profits by an increased salary, and the House of Correction was combined with the prison. In 1843 the governor Robert Andrews retired *'from Old age and Decrepitude'* and was given a pension of £150 p.a. – the first time that this had happened. His successor Charles Duke managed to maintain the 'family' connection by obtaining the post of matron for his wife (matrons had been employed since 1815). There were complaints about the Dukes and they were succeeded by another husband-and-wife team, the Lawrences, in 1848. Thereafter the posts were separated.

The post of prison chaplain became associated in the seventeenth century with the incumbent of the Dorchester parish of All Saints. In the 1680s there was concern that the Rev. Richard Pyne was neglecting his duties and the Rev. Peter Blanchard was appointed in 1690 at a salary of £20 p.a.

A hundred years later this had increased to £50 p.a., when the Rev. Thomas Bryer of Fordington became chaplain. Mr Bryer clearly thought that the inmates needed more spiritual support, because in 1787 he ordered a new Bible and some Books of Common Prayer, at a cost of £3 7s, from Messrs Gould and Thorne, booksellers of Dorchester.

A later chaplain was not giving satisfaction in 1821, when it was complained that the Rev. John Palmer was not filling in his journal as required by the prison rules. He resigned shortly afterwards and Quarter Sessions advertised the post.

A new chaplain, the Rev. George Wood, was elected by majority vote in January 1823. At the Easter Sessions that year a letter was read to the justices. It was from three men, Thomas Harvey, Thomas Dosseter and William Harvey, who had been executed at Dorchester on 29 March, expressing their appreciation of Mr Wood's kind endeavours on their behalf. Their crime had been burglary at the house of Lady Caroline Damer.

As in many other offices of the nineteenth century, incumbents tended to remain long. The Rev. Dacre Clemetson resigned as chaplain in 1860 after thirty-five years, on a pension of £166 13s 4d p.a. – two-thirds pay. The following year an attempt was made to pay the organist in the gaol chapel a salary of £10 p.a., but it was pointed out that to do so would break the law. An interesting survey made by the chaplain in 1863 indicated that of 833 prisoners admitted in the previous year, 419 could read and write, while a further 170 could read. Provision of elementary education for all children did not begin until 1870.

Until the 1770s the gaol surgeon was called and paid only when necessary. Thereafter the post entailed a regular part-time salary: Christopher Arden, surgeon and apothecary, was paid £30 p.a. in 1797, rising to £40 p.a. in 1801. Detailed reports begin to appear in the Quarter Sessions Order Book from 1804, with numbers of inmates indicated under the headings of *Fevers, Fluxes, and Other Complaints*. Another example of long incumbency occurred – in 1860 the gaol surgeon resigned after forty-nine years in office. His successor was paid £120 p.a.

The first mention of a gaol schoolmaster appears in 1825, an indication of concern about the low level of literacy among the very young prisoners, some of whom were under ten years of age. Thereafter there are occasional references and in 1847 a temporary schoolmaster acted as deputy governor of the prison when the officer was ill. In 1855 the schoolmaster's salary was fixed at £55 p.a., but ten years later it had reached £75 and the schoolmaster was promoted to deputy governor in 1870.

The provision of housing around the prison for governor, chaplain and 'turnkeys' (warders) began in the 1850s – the turnkeys' houses cost about £100 apiece.

Escapes

Escapes from the prison were mentioned in the Quarter Sessions record mainly when rewards were paid to those who recaptured the absconder. To hinder escapes all convicted felons had their clothes removed at night. 'Irons' or shackles were only used for very troublesome prisoners or those who had attempted to escape.

In 1837 the constable of Farringdon in Berkshire was paid five guineas for the apprehension of Eli Balson, who had escaped from Dorchester Gaol. Eight years later Samuel Champ, a Special Constable, pursued Harry Warr of Bridport, a forger, to the U.S.A., and was given £195 16s. 2d for his expenses.

At Easter 1861 Alfred Dicker was reported to have escaped, and this was blamed on the *'culpable conduct of Warder Pope who brought the prisoner outside the Gaol Door to unload a Coal Wagon'.*

Escapes were not frequent, though inevitably there were occasional lapses of security. The tale is told of an occasion in the 1970s when a prisoner on remand and therefore wearing his own clothes was brought down to the visiting room just inside the main gate to meet his family. When the visiting time was up the Gate Officer conducted the family out of the gate and locked it behind them. Twenty minutes later there was a ring at the bell, and he opened the door to see the prisoner standing there. *'Thank you very much'* said the prisoner, *'I've seen them off on the bus.'*

Recent Times

In the later twentieth century prison conditions improved nationally, with greater opportunities for education and training, but improvements were more difficult to achieve in Victorian gaols like Dorchester, which had been re-built when taken over by central government in 1880. Heating in winter was notoriously unreliable and dependent on how far cells were from the boiler. Gradually toilets in cells replaced the 'slopping-out' and sluices.

The library and later the permission for radio and even televisions in cells made the interminable hours behind locked doors more bearable. Memories of dirty cardboard boxes containing long-faded jigsaw puzzles supplied to illiterate inmates over weekends when they were 'banged-up' for twenty-three hours a day have faded – but prison is still a dire experience.

And Now?

The government ordered the closure of Dorchester Prison in 2013. For the first time in 700 years there is no gaol in the county town. The future of the site and buildings is yet unclear.

The Borough Prisons

For several hundred years most Dorset boroughs also had prisons or small lock-ups for short-term incarceration of petty criminals. These were under the control of the borough justices and town councils.

Poole had a substantial prison in King Street, built about 1800. Since Poole was also a county, the prison was in the charge of the sheriff, but the justices appointed the gaoler.

The prison contained six sleeping rooms or cells, with a day-room for the use of those imprisoned for debt. A single room operated as a House of Correction, where sentences of hard labour could be served and to that end there were a treadmill and labour-yard. An additional small lock-up existed near the quay, adjoining the town-cellars and this was known as the 'Salisbury'. By the 1830s Poole had regular policing by six daily constables and six nightly constables, so this little gaol did not lack for custom. In due course the police stations took over the functions of the local lock-ups.

31. Transportation and Penal Servitude

Since the Middle Ages defendants who could prove that they were in Holy Orders by reading a verse from the Bible could not be sentenced to loss of life or limb. This was known as benefit of clergy, and had largely become a legal fiction by the mid-seventeenth century and was to become more so. In the eighteenth century it was extended to women, in an even greater fiction, since they could not be clergy. The usual penalty which followed a successful claim was branding in the hand, on the basis that a second claim could not be made, as the transgressor would have been 'defrocked', ie lost his clerical status, after the first offence. Imprisonment was rarely imposed because prisons were regarded as places to keep defendants before punishment, not for punishment. Justices tended to feel that too many offenders were getting away with the brief pain of branding and that a more severe penalty short of hanging was desirable.

Transportation

The answer lay in transportation. Sending miscreants to labour-hungry colonies for unpaid service appealed to the instincts of magistrates. They could see retribution, protection of the public and training in habits of industry as an ideal disposal - and there was always the hope that the convict would never come back, even after his time had expired. In addition to these advantages, transportation was cheaper than hanging - the cost to the county was about five pounds whereas an execution might cost as much as six or seven pounds.

The first indication of transportation in the Dorset Quarter Sessions records is in September 1664, when a prisoner was ordered to be transported or to *'serve His Majesty at sea'*. Two years later five felons were sentenced to be branded in the

Prison hulk at Portsmouth.

hand, but respited because of their *'severall desires to be transported to some English Plantation beyond the Seas'*.

A Dorset magistrate Sir John Strode undertook the transportation at no cost to the county. Unkindly one wonders whether their destination was unpaid labour on his own estate in the colonies. These were not the only offenders to request transportation at this time, perhaps because of the lure of riches in the New World.

In July 1665 *'Bartholomew Tilling of Pullham in this County an idle and dangerous person being brought into this Courte having formerly byn in the house of Correction and was to have byn transported which was suspended in respect of his sicknesse and having now married a second wife, is complained of for endeavouring to destroy his child by his second wife in a most inhumane manner'*. He was remanded to the House of Correction and disappears from the record.

An Act of Parliament in 1718 regulated the system, but transportation was mainly a sentence of the Assize Court rather than Quarter Sessions, until the reduction of capital offences from the late eighteenth century gradually brought more business back to Quarter Sessions. However, instances occurred and the necessary arrangements had to be made. Sometimes these were left to the Clerk of the Peace, but in 1755 six justices (or any two of them) were nominated to make a contract with a suitable person to organise the transportation of John Senior to America for seven years. In 1771 James Chaffey, the gaolkeeper, was paid £5 5s for conveying Sarah Oldis to Bristol for transportation. The American Revolution upset the pattern, as the newly-independent United States quite naturally refused to accept British convicts. As a temporary measure, transportees were housed in old ships known as 'hulks', moored in the Thames and elsewhere.

In 1785 Batt Chaffey, who had succeeded his father as gaolkeeper in Dorchester, was paid £47 9s 6d for conveying six prisoners to the *Ceres* hulk at Woolwich, in the charge of Duncan Campbell Esq., the Overseer of Convicts in the River Thames. Presumably the prisoners did not have to walk because in 1799 Mr Lawrence King, carpenter and wheeler, was paid '*for making a new Waggon for the Conveyance of the Prisoners*'.

Australia provided the answer to the problem, and the first convict fleet set sail for Botany Bay in 1788.

The reforms of Sir Robert Peel as Home Secretary in the 1820s reduced the number of capital offences, though it was in the next decade that the drastic changes took place which altered the whole design of punishment. The death penalty disappeared for a host of offences, and by 1861 could only be inflicted for murder, treason, piracy and setting fire to a royal dockyard. The result was a surge of business for Quarter Sessions and a vast extension of transportation. In Dorset the most usual period of transportation in the early nineteenth century was seven years and it was given to both men and women.

Very serious offences could incur fourteen years or even life. Between 1827 and 1835 there were eighty-six transportation orders from Dorset Quarter Sessions alone – there were more from the judges, including in 1834 the Tolpuddle Martyrs. The rate increased in the next decade from an average of eleven to seventeen a year. In 1852 a housebreaker with previous convictions was transported for twenty years.

By this time there was great doubt about the system in the more liberal climate of opinion. New South Wales had effectively refused any more convicts, and Tasmania and Western Australia were the destinations chosen in the 1840s and 1850s.

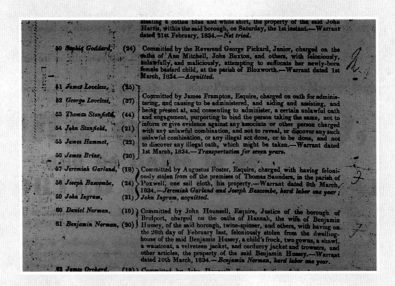

*Court record showing
transportation of the Tolpuddle
Martyrs in 1834.*

Gladstone as Home Secretary suspended transportation for a couple of years and it was finally abolished in 1857. Dorset magistrates were still enthusiastically transporting housebreakers when the last convict ship sailed: at Easter 1857 William Bartlett was given seven years.

Locking-up offenders as a punishment was largely confined to the House of Correction in Sherborne rather than the gaol in Dorchester, until the two institutions merged at the end of the eighteenth century. The original aim of the House of Correction under the Elizabethan Poor Law was the training of idle rogues in habits of industry and the improvement of the morals of unmarried mothers. Gradually the use of the institution for short periods of incarceration with 'hard labour' increased as a penalty for all kinds of petty offences.

Even so, numbers in the house at Sherborne remained small, usually around half-a-dozen. In 1754 there was something of a peak indicated in the Calendar, with fourteen inmates, though the magistrates immediately ordered seven of them to be whipped and discharged. Sentencing to imprisonment without hard labour still meant that the offender had to work, but would be paid a small allowance for doing so.

In the early days of the new prison in Dorchester at the beginning of the nineteenth century a number of trades were practised, but the installation of the treadmill in the 1820s made hard labour a reality. By this time Quarter Sessions were sentencing to periods of a year or more of hard labour for repeated felonies of a minor kind. In 1861 a shed was built at the prison in order that prisoners unable to mount the treadwheel could be forced to break stones.

Solitary confinement was a further refinement of punishment, in which the stated aim was to give the convict the opportunity to reflect upon and to regret his misdoings. In June 1836 Ann Stainer was imprisoned for two months and one week in each month was to be in solitary confinement. The daily diet for those so imprisoned was laid down by the court to be 1½lbs of bread, one quart of water and one pint of gruel at night. The practice continued and in 1862 the Inspector of Prisons reported unfavourably on the use of solitary confinement in 'the Dark Cell' in Dorchester Prison.

Penal Servitude

The real breakthrough into long-term imprisonment began in the 1850s with the ending of transportation. No longer able to dispatch serious offenders to the other side of the world, Quarter Sessions sent them to penal servitude.

Central government had been experimenting with large prisons for national use since the Napoleonic Wars. Long periods under strict regimes in harsh conditions were seen as both deterrent and reformatory and the ideas of thinkers and reformers like Jeremy Bentham were adapted according to cost. Establishments such as Millbank, Pentonville and Portland provided an alternative to the death penalty and transportation. Since they were controlled centrally, out of the hands of the magistrates, they also provided the Home Office with an opportunity to try out such schemes as the 'silent system' and the 'solitary system'. Both these systems were based on cutting off inmates from communication with other human beings for years at a time, while threatening withdrawal of food if they failed to complete tasks of grinding hard labour.

The aim was reflection, remorse and reform: the result was a remarkable number of mentally-ill and dangerous people. Meantime, the Penal Servitude Act of 1853 established the pattern and in September of that year the Dorset magistrates imposed the first such sentence of six years. The following year they mixed their sentences, transporting one individual for fifteen years for repeated larceny and sending eight men to penal servitude for offences such as housebreaking and horse-stealing.

Thereafter penal servitude became a regular feature in the court, with roughly the same incidence as transportation had had just before abolition, that is, about six in each year. In 1862 a man was sentenced to ten years, but generally life sentences were left to the Assizes: there were twelve in the year 1865.

In 1866 Mr Floyer, the chairman of Quarter Sessions, in his charge to the Grand Jury referred to the large number of discharged convicts then at large in this country: as many as 21,052 compared with 1338 in 1854. He looked back to *'former times, when the great bulk of our convicts, after their sentences of transportation had expired, remained in the colonies.'* However, the Chief Constable reported that most ex-convicts were earning their living honestly. One who clearly wasn't was Daniel Carew, who was sentenced to seven years penal servitude in 1865, having been given four years penal servitude in 1855, and whipped a few years earlier.

In the 1870s a pattern of sentence familiar in our own day was adopted in Quarter Sessions, when a sentence of penal servitude or imprisonment was followed by the imposition of a period of supervision. In this case, however, the supervision was by the police, though in some respects it must have been comparable with today's supervision by the Probation Service. In January 1871, Sarah Westwood was sentenced to five years penal servitude followed by seven years police supervision, for the crime of false pretences.

32. Other Dorset Prisons

Portland Prison and the Young Offender Institution

Portland Prison was an experiment by central government, far removed from the development of the County Gaol in Dorchester. It was created for two reasons: first, to provide a preliminary stage for the assessment of men sentenced to transportation to Australia; and second, to act as a permanent reservoir of labour for the immense task of the construction of Portland Breakwater.

The first convicts arrived in 1848, and were housed in wooden shacks. Initially they were employed to build the permanent accommodation, but before long were hewing and transporting the great loads of stone for the naval establishment of Portland Harbour. The prison was designed to hold several hundred men in massive stone blocks which are still in use today. The punishment of transportation was abolished in the late 1850s, so inmates often endured many years of hard labour in the quarries.

The regime at Portland was severe, and most of the prisoners were hardened criminals. Some were better-educated and were paying the price for such crimes as fraud. One of the best-known was Jabez Balfour, a former MP, who later described Portland as 'a heart-breaking, soul-enslaving, brain-destroying hell upon earth'.

In 1922 the prison was converted to a 'Borstal', the name given to training establishments for young boys guilty of serious offences. The length of sentences was not fixed but depended on the assessment of improved behaviour and attitude. Strong emphasis was placed on education and physical training, but the structure of the prison retained the landings and locked cells as

*The gate of Portland Prison,
early twentieth century.*

before. The advent of the Young Offender Institution in the 1980s returned to the system of fixed sentences. Recently some adult offenders have been placed at the YOI.

The Verne Prison

The Verne Citadel was a huge fortification built on Portland heights in the 1840s to defend the new naval anchorage created by Portland Breakwater. For a century it was part of a system of South Coast defences mainly designed to prevent invasion by the French, though latterly the enemy was Germany.

After World War Two, with Germany defeated and Anglo-French relations more amicable, the Citadel was no longer cost-effective, and in 1949 it was converted to a prison for adult males. The huge walls now turned round in effect – keeping people in rather than out. This security was quite successful, and there were very few escapes. Attempts to climb over the walls usually failed, and sometimes the prison hospital had patients suffering from 'Verne Ankle', a fracture resulting from falling from a great height.

The Verne Prison offered training for various trades, together with the opportunity for further education, but the proportion of foreign prisoners reached more than 60%, and there were 50 different nationalities among the population of about 600. Conditions within the walls were much more relaxed than in many prisons since escape was so difficult: inmates were issued with keys to their own rooms – not cells – in accommodation blocks, and there were good facilities for recreation and sport. Most of the inmates were serving long sentences or even life.

Portland Breakwater,
constructed by convict labour.

In 2013 the government announced the closure of the Verne Prison, and the conversion of the site for the housing of illegal immigrants.

Guy's Marsh

Just south of Shaftesbury is Guy's Marsh Prison. Originally it was an American military hospital during and after World War Two, but in 1960 the site was taken over for use as a Borstal Institution for training young offenders. Effectively it was a large camp with single storey accommodation and limited security where suitable boys could be offered useful education and skills. Gradually the security was increased, and in 1984 the regime of a Young Offender Institution with fixed sentences was introduced. A few years later the admission of some adult offenders began, and the last young men were removed in 2008. The establishment is now a secure training prison for adults.

The Prison Ship

The great increase in the prison population in the late twentieth century created accommodation problems across the country. One expedient was the use of a prison ship which was moored alongside in Portland Harbour in 1997, and was named *Weare*. The very thought conjured up folk-memories of wooden hulks in the Thames and at Portsmouth to house convicts awaiting transportation to the penal colonies, and there was great political and social opposition.

HMP *Weare* was a floating barracks, which had been used variously as accommodation for construction workers as well as a prison. About 400 men were held there on several decks, controlled by substantial prison staff. There were few facilities and conditions were heavily criticised by the Inspectorate. Indeed the Chief Inspector Ann Owers described *Weare* as 'literally and metaphorically a container'. Eventually it closed in 2005 and the barge was sold to a Nigerian oil company to house its operatives.

33. Probation

The idea of 'probation' as an alternative to punishment began with the work of voluntary 'Police Court Missionaries' in the late nineteenth century. To more socially-aware magistrates, petty criminals often seemed to be more in need of guidance than retribution, and the justices began to postpone sentencing while entrusting the offender to the care of such missionaries.

In many courts very short sentences of imprisonment had seemed the only suitable punishment when clearly fines would not be paid, but it became obvious that such disposals were ineffective and often counter-productive: training-courses in criminal skills provided by experienced inmates.

From 1907 it became lawful for courts to appoint paid Probation Officers, and Bournemouth did so with Captain Frank Barrett of Boscombe Salvation Army in 1908. The Dorset county magistrates were slower off the mark, but in 1925 the Criminal Justice Act required the establishment of Probation Committees by the separate Benches. In 1937 these were combined into a County Committee. Until then only one Probation Officer had been employed full-time for the whole county, supported by a team of part-timers and volunteers.

The committee was informed in 1940 that at Blandford
'Miss M.E. Weston has acted as part-time Probation Officer at £10pa for many years, and although now over 80 years of age and practically bed-ridden, she still takes an active interest in Probation work and often interviews cases at her home.'

During World War Two and afterwards the Probation Service expanded dramatically in answer to the social problems thrown up or highlighted by the emergency. By the 1970s the attitudes among younger Probation Officers across the country in favour of political and social reform began to spill over into their

Unpaid Community Service.

work. Even in Dorset magistrates became restive in the face of what seemed to be constant pressure for leniency.

A huge extension of probation responsibilities and facilities such as the supervision of Community Service and the provision of Probation Hostels and Centres, were aimed at the reduction of crime and the lowering of the prison population. Probation Hostels were opened in Weymouth and Boscombe, together with a Probation Centre at Bournemouth and then Parkstone. These aims were not achieved and for a while crime rates continued to rise. In the last years of the twentieth century government policy was to direct probation towards the intensive supervision of more serious offenders after imprisonment, on the basis that the social work to help petty offenders was not cost-effective. This meant a radical change in the ethos of probation, which many officers found difficult. The County Probation Services were merged into a National Service, and magistrates no longer held responsibility.

And yet – the level of crime has gone down in the first decades of the twenty-first century. This is reflected across the Western World, and so far no single reason can be established.

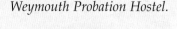

Weymouth Probation Hostel.

34. Juvenile Offenders

Until the nineteenth century children were tried for offences in the same way as adults, and the age for criminal responsibility from the twelfth century onwards was seven years. (This was raised to eight in 1933 and ten in 1963.) Until the early nineteenth century children as young as nine were tried at the Assizes and even hanged – the last time seems to have been as late as 1831, though this was not in Dorset. Transportation of children continued until the 1850s. Penal reformers had been calling for a more humane approach to young offenders since the late eighteenth century and some attempts were made in various parts of the country to provide schemes such as farm colonies. The Juvenile Offenders Act of 1847 allowed children under fourteen charged with larceny to be tried summarily by two magistrates, without a jury, rather than Quarter Sessions.

The first important advance took place in 1854, when Parliament allowed offending juveniles under sixteen to be sent to reformatory schools. The schools were established on a charitable basis and counties would make a contribution for each child sent.

The earliest use of this facility made by Dorset Quarter Sessions was in 1856, when George Husher was convicted of false pretences and was sentenced to fourteen days' hard labour and two years in the Devon Reformatory School. A year later Francis Greening received five months' hard labour and was sent to the Dorset Reformatory: the first mention of this institution. Thereafter similar sentences are regular, with the period in prison to comply with the Act usually short, but the period in the reformatory often extended to the full five years permitted. An under-sixteen year old boy convicted of shoplifting was given a whipping as well for good measure in 1860.

In 1858 a committee was appointed to arrange with Devon and Exeter Female Reformatory School, for female juvenile offenders from Dorset to be received at a total cost not to exceed £300 per year. In the summer of 1860 Ann Reed and Louisa Reed were duly sentenced to two years there. Perhaps they were difficult pupils, because in 1862 the Devon Reformatory asked for an increased contribution – which was indignantly refused! A decision was made in 1869 to send girls to Limpley Stoke Reformatory near Bath.

The provision of Industrial Schools was allowed under the Act of 1857. These schools gave training to children in need of care, but were not reformatories and it was not necessary to commit a crime to be sent there. The Rev. Carr John Glyn had often spoken in Dorset Quarter Sessions of the advantages of such schools and in 1872 the Order Book records his *'munificent spirit'* in establishing an Industrial School and Reformatory School for girls at Poole. The hope was expressed that some gentleman would give an Industrial School for boys, there already being a Reformatory at Milborne.

Later that year attention was drawn to the Bristol Training Ship *Formidable* for Homeless and Destitute Boys, and Quarter Sessions agreed to pay one shilling per week for each boy sentenced to be kept in such a ship. The same amount was to be paid to Poole Industrial School for each girl, but eleven years later and without explanation, it was recorded in the Order Book that girls could now be sent to St Margaret's Industrial School at Mill Hill near London by both County and Borough justices, at a cost of two shillings a week.

In 1875 there was a debate about the period in prison required by Act of Parliament before any young person convicted could be sent to one of the schools. Some thought it should be at least a month, presumably to impress on the miscreants the seriousness of their offences, but others, including Mr Glyn, thought prison reinforced their evildoing. The Industrial School at Poole took girls from seven to fourteen, together with refractory children from workhouses and *'pauper schools'*. It was pointed out that the only way to send offenders without the prison sentence was not to convict them in the first place!

A Victorian ragamuffin.

Poor country children in Dorset.

General concern at the plight of street children appears in 1877, when it was reported to Quarter Sessions that children were *'being imported from Italy and elsewhere into this Country by certain persons who send them into the streets to earn money by playing musical instruments, selling images etc.'*

A few months later the Rev. C.J. Glyn succeeded in getting the court to appoint a committee with himself as chairman to look into the provision by the county of an Industrial School for boys. Presumably the hopes of 1872, that 'some gentleman' would come forward to provide, had come to nothing. Forty-six boys were duly reported by Mr Glyn in the summer of 1878 as being in need of a training school, but he also mentioned that there was space available on a training ship at Plymouth. The matter was frequently discussed, but in the summer of 1879 objections were raised by the Cerne Poor Law Union, who said that the increased rates which would be necessary could not be afforded in the present depressed state of agriculture. At the Michaelmas Sessions it was suggested that the Milborne Reformatory School should be converted into an Industrial School, since at that time few boys were being committed there.

A letter from the Home Office in 1880 concerning the imprisonment of young offenders and how to avoid it may have had some influence, because it was announced in September 1881 that the Milborne Industrial School was now open. Justices in the various boroughs as well as the county were permitted to send boys to Milborne from 1882.

It was not until the late nineteenth century that society came to understand the need to deal separately with miscreant children. In 1879 it was made possible for children under the age of twelve charged with indictable offences to be tried by magistrates, rather than in the even more frightening circumstances of the Assizes with judge and jury.

The real breakthrough (as with so many other fundamental reforms), came with the Liberal government 1906-1914. The Children Act of 1908 set up separate juvenile courts, where proceedings were to be more informal and the public excluded. Children under fourteen were not to go to prison and those awaiting sentence were to be kept in Remand Homes: in Dorset this often meant the homes of Probation Officers.

In 1933 the Children and Young Persons Act established the Care Order, by which children could be sent by magistrates to the care of the Local Authority, or to an Approved School. The age of criminal responsibility was increased from seven to eight (in 1963 to ten years). The justices sitting in juvenile courts were elected by their bench and in 1948 it was recommended that they should be appointed in their thirties and must retire at sixty-five. After 1954 a juvenile bench had to include at least one man and one woman.

Dorset magistrates sent between ten and thirty (almost entirely boys) each year to Approved Schools, which were seen as providing good practical education and firm discipline. Some were reasonably successful, but two out of three boys re-offended soon after release. Fear of authority diminished substantially in the 1950s and unruly pupils became increasingly difficult to handle.

Belief that a better approach would be by kindness and understanding gradually developed and this was given immense impetus when a scandal of brutality resulted in the closure of the notorious Court Lees School in 1967. The result was the Children and Young Persons Act of 1969, when Approved Schools were abolished and Supervision Orders with Intermediate Treatment introduced. Almost all juvenile offenders were now to be supervised by the Social Services departments of Local Authorities, rather than Probation Officers.

Detention Centres for serious or frequent offenders from fourteen to twenty-one years had been set up in 1948, but in the late '70s became the subject of an experiment with the 'short sharp shock' – a few weeks of intensive and rigorous physical training and discipline. The trial did not last very long – it became apparent that the regime was popular with the miscreants as well as the vengeful public. To survive the Detention Centre was a badge of honour among peers and rates of re-offending did not diminish. It was also apparent to a group of magistrates from Dorset visiting a Detention Centre in Hampshire that at least some of the staff were clearly enjoying the opportunity to exercise their power. The Young Offender Institutions replaced both the Youth Custody Centres (ex-Borstals) and the Detention Centres in the 1980s.

The true extent of juvenile crime is unknown, but the desire in the last thirty years to keep as many children as possible out of the criminal justice system has made it even more difficult to assess the juvenile proportion of crime as a whole. The growth of widespread and repeated cautioning by the police has meant a substantial decrease in the business of juvenile courts, even in periods of rising crime. At times in the late '80s juvenile panels of rural benches did not sit at all for months on end, because there was nothing for them to do.

A further reduction in work occurred when, in the Children Act of 1989, all care proceedings were transferred to the new Family Court. The obvious solution was for benches to amalgamate their panels: this was the precursor of amalgamations of Petty Sessional Divisions. There is now one Combined Youth Court for the whole of Dorset.

From April 2013 the Youth Justice System became part of the Public Health England department of government. In Dorset there are two Youth Offending Teams, one for the county and the other for Bournemouth and Poole. Each of these teams has representatives from Social Services, Dorset Police, the Probation Service and the National Health Service. The teams are responsible for recommending appropriate action to the Youth Court.

Most children whose offences warrant more than a fine or discharge are placed in the care of Social Services, which may mean continuing to live in their own homes. Further crimes may result in a Residential Care Order, but the well-known problem of the lack of secure accommodation for the unredeemed serial offender led to the plan for Secure Children's Homes, Secure Training Establishments for young people between twelve and fifteen, and Young Offender Institutions for fifteen to eighteen-year-olds.

35. Policing Dorset

Maintaining law and order in Dorset, as in the rest of England, was in the hands of amateurs until the mid-nineteenth century and the reign of Queen Victoria. The word 'police' was not much used, and indeed suggested the tyranny of absolute monarchies across Europe.

Instead 'The Peace' depended on compulsory unpaid work by more or less reluctant male members of the community. High Constables in the ancient local areas known as 'hundreds', Petty Constables in the parishes and Tithingmen in the even smaller 'tithings', were annually elected or appointed and held to account by the justices for carrying out the orders of Quarter Sessions, executing warrants, arresting and conveying miscreants and organising punishments as appropriate. Those who took office were usually above the lowest social rank and often had experience of other similarly elective functions such as churchwardens and overseers of the poor.

The system was not very efficient and much crime went undetected and unpunished: but for rural communities it appeared adequate, in that it was cheap and bore heavily on no-one, and crime was not unduly oppressive. Some crimes that would be considered very serious today were matters where public sympathy lay with the offender: smuggling appealed to all classes, as indeed did the looting of wrecks. Poaching, in which class antipathy played a large part, was rather different.

The first cries for a professional police force came from middle-class Londoners in the eighteenth century, as it became clear that the threat of the death-penalty for more than two hundred types of crime was not having the desired effect. Parts of London were out of control and some of the new industrial cities were going the same way. Resistance to professional police came mainly from country gentry, who saw a curb on their freedom and a weapon for the tyranny of central government, together with increased rates. Since it was the country gentry who dominated the House of Commons, it was not until the last days of pre-reform government in 1829 that the Home Secretary, Robert Peel, was able to institute the Metropolitan Police in London.

The small towns across the country had always relied on 'the Watch' for keeping the peace. This amounted to a roster of householders who took turns to patrol the streets at night. The better-off usually paid substitutes to do the duty for them, and these were often old or disabled men whose watchkeeping was extremely poor.

Apparently this did not matter very much for several hundred years. Of course there was theft, drunkenness and violence, but most of it was minor, and people were used to taking the law into their own hands and meting out punishment themselves.

In 1835 all boroughs and corporate towns were required to establish their own police, so the Dorset boroughs were forced to act. For example, a Dorchester Police Force was set up, which consisted of six constables.

One was appointed superintendent. Only one officer was to have day duty, and the other five were to patrol the streets at night. Each man was supplied with a staff of office, a rattle, a stout walking stick and a lantern. A uniform based on that of the Metropolitan Police was provided, and the pay was to be two shillings (10p) per night.

A Watchhouse was established, and the Blind House was to continue as a lock-up. A book was kept in which officers were required to sign in and off, and to record any incidents, and the book was to be presented to the Town Clerk each morning. Although the force increased slightly, the essentials remained the same for half a century. In 1857 a Dorset County Police Force was created, more than a hundred strong, but Dorchester rejected the offer of their services and kept the Borough Police for another thirty years.

Dorset County Police Headquarters – late nineteenth century.

There was an impression in the 1830s that crime was spreading into the countryside from the urban areas: perhaps the London 'bobbies', the fast stage-coach lines and the early railways all helped to displace criminal activity! A reformed and reforming Parliament passed an Act in 1839 permitting Quarter Sessions to set up police districts, appoint chief constables and employ paid policemen under rules for pay and uniforms approved by the Home Secretary.

Dorset felt that the county had managed well enough with the traditional system. At difficult times, such as the rowdy elections of 1831, special constables had been recruited and were paid 3s a day. The specials were issued with decorated staves, which cost £5 ·6s 6d, and were stored for future use in 1833.

Accordingly Quarter Sessions passed a resolution:
'That although we have reason to lament the County of Dorset is not exempt from an increase of Crime which is found to have extended in a lamentable degree throughout almost every part of the Kingdom yet we are not satisfied that the increase of Crime is attributable to the insufficiency of the Constabulary force within this County... ' and therefore there was no need to recommend an expensive change.

Perhaps Weymouth Races in 1844 had some effect on opinion. The cost of employing special constables was considerable, and justices commented on the *'want of power of the Magistrates to check the nuisance now prevailing at Fairs and Races in consequence of the want of power to enforce the closing of Booths when liquor is sold at proper hours.'*

The first regular paid police force in the county of Dorset (excluding the boroughs) was set up in Sturminster Newton in 1849. Though it might seem that Sturminster was an unlikely hotbed of crime, the magistrates clearly felt it was necessary and John Hammond was appointed as superintendent at a salary of £100 p.a. and he was provided with a house.

The following year five paid constables were appointed for the Shaftesbury Division and the force was consolidated with that of Sturminster. The Shaftesbury Borough Police – two constables and a sergeant – joined in 1851.Wimbome Division followed in 1855, Blandford early in 1856.

Later that year an Act of Parliament made it compulsory for every county to have a police force and the Dorset County Police were established. A County Police Committee of 13 justices was appointed to supervise the force. Initially police strength was to be one hundred and twelve.

In September 1856 Lieut. Col. S. Cox was appointed chief constable and approved by the Home Secretary; he served for eleven years. Funds were provided for police stations, and where possible these were to be combined with rooms for Petty Sessional Courts. A new chief constable in 1867, Captain Amyatt Brown, introduced a new uniform. The tall hat and frock coat were replaced by a helmet and tunic, with the approval of Quarter Sessions.

The County Police established their Headquarters in a large new Police Station in Weymouth Avenue, built in 1860 and still there today – though now only a part-time local station. The Dorchester Borough Police finally merged with the County Police in 1890.

The subject of alleged police brutality, not unfamiliar in our own day, came up in 1870, when the Rev. John Hiley Austen complained at Quarter Sessions of the harsh treatment of some gypsies encamped on the roadside adjoining his lands. However, inspections by the Home Office were satisfactory, the force was pronounced to be efficient and one quarter of the cost of the police was paid from government funds. In 1888 Quarter Sessions lost its control, which was vested in a Standing Joint Committee of the Justices and the newly-established County Council. In 2012 this Dorset Police Authority was replaced by an elected Police and Crime Commissioner.

In the late twentieth century County Police Headquarters moved to Winfrith, and there are several substantial Divisional HQs. How would the watchmen of 1836 have reacted to the idea of a helicopter crew performing their nightly patrols?

CONCLUSION

There is, of course, no conclusion. This is a continuing story in which the details of crime and punishment change, but the theme remains the same: the 'cure' for crime has not been discovered. The struggle goes on because society cannot exist in anarchy. Simple 'solutions' of the 'hang'em and flog'em' variety do not work because they have been tried and because a civilised society cannot tolerate them. Experiments involving people who call for more severe punishment usually find that when they are faced with the facts and the background of a case, the hangers and floggers 'pass' sentences more lenient than those actually given in court.

Dorset is one of the more peaceful parts of the country, and the crime rate is low. We cannot be complacent, and must continue to support community efforts to Keep the Peace.